GATEWAY

To the Christian College Experience

J. Randolph Turpin, Jr.

DECLARATION PRESS

Gateway to the Christian College Experience
Copyright © 2015 by J. Randolph Turpin, Jr.
All Rights Reserved

This material may not be reproduced in any form
without the expressed written permission
of the author.

Scriptures taken from the Holy Bible, New International Version®, NIV®.
Copyright © 1973, 1978, 1984, 2011 by Biblica, Inc.™
Used by permission of Zondervan. All rights reserved worldwide.
www.zondervan.com
The "NIV" and "New International Version" are trademarks registered in the
United States Patent and Trademark Office by Biblica, Inc.™

Second Printing

Contents

Preface		1
Introduction		3
Chapter 1	Your Story	5
Chapter 2	Your College	21
Chapter 3	Your Calling	45
Chapter 4	Your Goals and Plans	57
Chapter 5	Attitudes for Success	65
Chapter 6	Managing Yourself	77
Chapter 7	Best Academic Practices	93
Chapter 8	Your Learning Style	111
Chapter 9	Relationships	119
Chapter 10	Finishing Strong	149

Preface

The first thought of creating this textbook / workbook came as I was teaching my second semester of Success in College—a gateway course at Valor Christian College in Columbus, Ohio. I felt that our entry-level students needed some basics that were not being addressed in the text the college was using at the time, and much of what I was personally generating as supplementary material was becoming the most helpful content of the course. Compiling and integrating that material within the formation of a new book seemed the best way to get this material into the mainstream of work for the class. Thus was the genesis of what will hopefully be the first of several editions.

Because I desire to connect with students conversationally as a mentor would speak to a mentee, for this publication I have chosen to write in the first and second person. Such informality is not typical for a college textbook; therefore, as a student, do not interpret my writing style as implied permission to compose your college papers informally as well.

Actually, you will discover that this volume is more of a workbook than a textbook. While it does contain content to be read and studied, these pages also include sections calling for your contribution of information and personal reflections. In the college where I am currently teaching, I originally required this work from my students as a series of written assignments. That approach was far too demanding for both the student and the instructor. The grading of six papers per student multiplied by fifty students each semester was a bit overwhelming! This approach is better.

Gateway to the Christian College Experience

The preparation of this edition of *Gateway* was informed by feedback from the alpha-test of a pre-release version in my Success in College class at Valor Christian College. I am especially grateful to the students who participated in the Fall 2015 Semester: Charles Amissah, Al Battle, Cassidy Brinkley, Passion Coleman, Isaiah Cress, Weston Dalton, Jazmin Dandridge, Yvenson Desgranges, Richard Devotie, Trevor Dishmond, Darshan Duckson, Faith Foulks, Angelica Gatchell, Kurtlando Gordon, Tyler Hamilton, Kalah Hatfield, Joshua Jarrell II, Charity Kopshina, Jacqueline Kopshina, Alexandria Lee, Daniel Logo, Joshua Maxwell, Credel McKnight, Junia Montaie, Jeremiah Patterson, Nathaniel Rodriguez, Antonio Sawyer-Hodge, Ashkell Smith, Salome Stephenson, Jesse Thao, Ross Van Reenan, Hannah Vance, Jehvona Whatley and Dorian Williams.

This text will typically be used in conjunction with instructor-guided coursework. As the author, I consider myself an invisible companion with you and your instructor in this orientation to the Christian college experience. Thank you for including me in your journey!

J. Randolph Turpin, Jr.
Canal Winchester, Ohio
November 16, 2015

Introduction

Welcome to college! You have chosen to attend a *Christian* college. This school is not just religious; it is *Christian*, identifying itself with the living reality of the Lord Jesus Christ. Who Jesus is, what Jesus said, what Jesus did, and what Jesus is still doing are essential to this institution's mission. The fact that you have made this school your educational choice implies that you also desire to hold to the centrality of Christ as you prepare for your personal life-mission.

Your professors are devoted to setting you up for success, but *you* are responsible for your own success. They should not have to work harder for your success than you. Draw upon their wisdom. Take advantage of the opportunities set before you. Utilize college learning resources as they are made available. Apply yourself to your educational and vocational pursuit with a spirit of excellence. Once again, *you* are responsible for your own success.

Each chapter of this text will sequentially lead you toward crafting a plan for success in college. In chapter one, you will reflect on "Your Story" with a view toward discovering the goodness of God in your life. In chapter two, you will be introduced to "Your College"—an overview assignment that your instructor may choose to spread out over two weeks. Chapter three, "Your Calling," and chapter four, "Your Goals and Plans," will help you compose a personalized plan for the college journey. Chapter five deals with "Attitudes for Success," promoting the breaking of self-imposed limitations and the cultivation of victorious mindsets. Chapter six, "Managing Yourself," and chapter seven, "Best Academic Practices," address practical matters related to living the life of a college student. In chapter eight, you will identify "Your Learning Style." Chapter nine highlights the importance of

"Relationships" at this point in your life, and chapter ten will deal with the practical aspects of "Finishing Strong" as you approach the conclusion of the school term.

As you enter the gateway to the Christian college experience, remember these encouraging words that the Apostle Paul wrote to the Philippians: "He who began a good work in you will carry it on to completion until the day of Christ Jesus."[1]

---

[1] Philippians 1:6.

Chapter 1
Your Story

You have a story to tell that only you can tell. You came into this world for a purpose—to fulfill a mission that is uniquely yours. God has met you at many points in your life-journey, and with each God-encounter, He has inscribed something more of His message upon your life. It is *your* story coupled with *His* story. In fact, you have become a part of His story. Become aware of that story, and at appropriate moments, tell that story.

A new chapter has begun. You have arrived at a Christian college, and you are here for a God-ordained purpose. New relationships are about to be formed. New experiences, challenges and blessings await you. The many episodes of your life leading up to this moment have prepared you for what is about to unfold. At this moment, you may *not* feel prepared; nevertheless, God in His sovereignty *has* been at work imparting that which is needed into your life.

Personal Introductions

In your first class session, it is likely that some time will be given to personal introductions. Your instructor will introduce himself or herself, and you will exchange initial greetings with other members of the class as well. When you introduce yourself to people around you, that small introductory segment of your story connects them with the larger picture of what God is doing. Likewise, as you pay attention to what they have to say, you will gain the benefit of their words. The sharing of our stories with one another promotes mutual understanding and draws us into a greater awareness of how God is at work in the midst of us.

Before we delve into the deeper aspects of your story, take some time to share something about yourself on an introductory level. Complete the following exercise in preparation for introducing yourself to others in class.

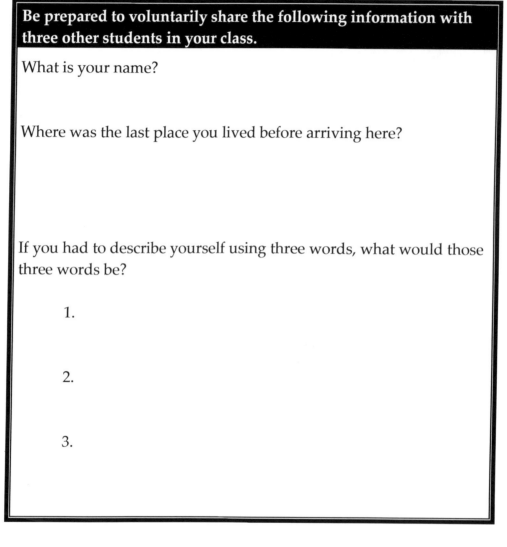

> **Be prepared to voluntarily share the following information with three other students in your class.**
>
> What is your name?
>
> Where was the last place you lived before arriving here?
>
> If you had to describe yourself using three words, what would those three words be?
>
>   1.
>
>   2.
>
>   3.

When your teacher instructs you to do so, share what you have written with two or three other members of your class. Then carefully listen to what they have to share. As you listen, jot down a few notes in the spaces that follow.

Your Story

What did other students share with you during this personal introduction time?

1st Student's Name: _____

    Where he/she lived before arriving here:

    Three words the student used to describe himself/herself:

        1.

        2.

        3.

2nd Student's Name: _____

    Where he/she lived before arriving here:

    Three words the student used to describe himself/herself:

        1.

        2.

        3.

3rd Student's Name: _____

    Where he/she lived before arriving here:

    Three words the student used to describe himself/herself:

        1.

        2.

        3.

Gateway to the Christian College Experience

Hopefully by listening to one another, you are starting to build some new relationships in this college environment.

Discovering God in Your Journey

You will discover more about God by reflecting on the story of your life-journey. The Bible repeatedly reveals that God is good.[2] In what ways have you encountered His goodness along the way? What have you seen, heard[3] or experienced? What have you learned about Him?

List five evidences of God's goodness that you have encountered in your life.
1.
2.
3.
4.
5.

---

[2] 1 Chronicles 16:34; Psalm 107:1; 118:1; 136:1.

[3] Acts 4:20.

Your Story

What have you learned about God through your encounters with His goodness?

Take a few moments to share with one other person your response to the preceding two exercises.

Life's Questions

The questions of life pull us deeper into the knowledge of God. The progression of our life-story with its highs and lows causes questions to surface. Where do we go to find the answers? As Christians, we often go to God's story—what we know about Him from the Bible—to find the answers. The answers that we discover then become part of each of our personal stories. In fact, the answers that we discover and incorporate into our lives become part of our theology. If it were not for the things that we have experienced, some things would be missing from our belief system. While we should not base our doctrines and beliefs on experience alone, experiences do influence the way that we think about God and the world around us. Experiences create a lens through which we see things.

For instance, people who have experienced a life of prosperity and peace do not have the same questions as people who have experienced much poverty and suffering. People who have suffered and people who have not experienced much suffering will ask different questions. Our beliefs are largely developed around the questions that we ask.

Consider another example. People who have experienced the miraculous power of God will have a different understanding of God and His ways. I may read about miracles in the Bible, but when I experience miracles, I can talk about my theology of miracles with greater clarity, authority and conviction.

Let us look at another example. A person who is an orphan—one who has lost a father or mother—will understand God as Father in a different way. Can you see how our experiences affect the way we theologize?

So, your personal story is a major factor in the process of theologizing—the building of your faith. Theology is not just about reading the Bible and saying, "This is what the Bible says." That is good, and that is a correct practice, but reciting the Bible is not the only function or concern of theology. Theology is more personal than that. It is about *knowing God*. It is not just important to learn how the Gospel writer Matthew experienced Christ. It is not just important to learn how the Apostle John experienced Christ. It is not just important to learn how the Apostle Paul and the Gentile churches experienced Christ. *I* need to experience Christ. *I* need to know Him. *You* need to experience Christ. *You* need to know Him.

Journaling

If you base your thoughts about God on a single snapshot of what He *is* or *is not* doing in your life on any particular day, you will have a limited perspective of Him. Life is more like a movie than a snapshot. This movie is your story, and it has a beginning, middle and end. You are not at the beginning, and you are not at the end. You are somewhere in the middle. Outcomes are yet to be seen. Rightly discerning what God is doing in your life requires reflecting on where you have been and envisioning where you are going.

If you are not already doing so, consider starting a personal journal. Each day record your reflections on God's Word and the things you are experiencing. Write down what He is speaking to you and showing you. Envision where you want to go, what you want to do and the kind of person you hope to become. Jot down those thoughts.

Life brings to each of us both positive and negative experiences. If you are writing about something of a negative nature, make sure that you include redemptive insights regarding the matter. This practice could prove especially helpful while you are on your journey through college. On some days you may do exceptionally well in your studies, in social situations and in spiritual matters. On other days you may not be doing so well. Whichever is the case, what is God doing in the midst of it all? If things are going favorably for you, express your gratitude to God in your writing. If things are not going favorably, express your trust in God, and praise Him anyhow! Get in the practice of incorporating what Scripture has to say about your struggles. Doing so will help to create mental patterns that will orient your mind in a positive direction.

Over time the written account of your life will reveal consistent and reoccurring patterns of the sovereign hand of God in your life. *His* story will begin to unfold within *your* story. In years to come, you will review what you have written and be reminded of the constancy of God's love and faithfulness.

Envisioning Your Future

By reflecting on your past and present, you can discern clues for the future direction of your life. What have been the reoccurring incidents of God's goodness in your life? What evidences of grace keep showing up over and over again? Do you see any patterns with these factors? What people has He used repeatedly in your journey to speak wisdom into your life? What have they said? What prophetic words have you received? What themes from the Bible keep speaking to you? What particular talents, gifts and skills do you have that repeatedly produce something beneficial for others? What makes you happy? What are your dreams for your future—those hopeful thoughts that keep coming back to you? Answers to questions such as these may prove helpful for envisioning goals for your future. Of a more immediate concern, answers to such questions can help you set goals for your college experience, and you will be given the opportunity to do so later in this workbook.

The Power of Testimony

Out of your life-story, a powerful testimony is emerging. In every instance where you have encountered God, an empowering grace has been deposited into your life that has left you forever changed. The grace that you experience today can remain upon you for years to come; you actually carry it for the benefit of others. The telling of your testimony is a way of stewarding that grace.

The Hebrew word for "testimony" or "witness" comes from a word meaning "to give evidence." At its primitive root, the word means "to repeat, to do again." Testimony brings that past event into the present as though it were happening again—as though it were being reenacted in full view of your hearers.

Testimony increases the likelihood that the encounter or miracle will happen again. When you share your testimony, you are *inviting* God to do it again. You are announcing that God is present to do it again. When you hear a testimony, recognize that it is an invitation from God for you to step into the realm of His goodness in that same area in your life. For instance, if another student shares a testimony of how God restored his or her self-confidence, believe that God can do the same thing for you. In a sense, when you hear a testimony, you can reach out and take it. It is for you.

When a person shares a testimony about a particular outcome, God actually allows you to imitate that person's faith! Consider these words from the book of Hebrews:

> Remember your leaders, who spoke the word of God to you. Consider the outcome of their way of life and imitate their faith. Jesus Christ is the same yesterday and today and forever.[4]

Can one person actually imitate another person's faith? When I hear another person tell their story about how faith in Christ has made a difference in their life, I want to imitate their faith. When I imitate their faith, I can expect Jesus to be just as faithful in my situation as He was in the situation of the person whose testimony I have heard. Why do I have that expectation? I have that expectation because of Hebrews 13:8 that says, "Jesus Christ is the same yesterday and today and forever." What He has done before, He can do again. Another person's testimony of faith inspires me to have faith, and Jesus will respond to my faith just like He responded to the other person's faith.

When I was ten years old I heard another ten-year-old boy deliver a testimony of how he gave his life to Jesus. I said in my heart, "If he can give his life to Jesus, I can give my life to Jesus too." The altar call was given, I went forward, and I gave my life to Jesus that night. I was

---

[4] Hebrews 13:7-8.

imitating the faith of that other ten-year-old child. His testimony was simple, yet powerful.

A few years ago in an evening service at the church I was pastoring in Maine, a teenage girl experienced an instantaneous healing of a severe eyesight disorder. She shared her testimony with the congregation the following Sunday. Immediately after the testimony, a middle-age woman stood to her feet believing that God could heal her eyes too. Jesus instantly delivered her from a similar eyesight condition! Several months later I shared both of those accounts with a group of pastors at a seminary in Haiti, and while hearing those testimonies one pastor exercised his faith believing that God could do the same for him. Within moments he came forward having just received the ability to read the small print in his Bible for the first time! Glory to God!

The Bible contains numerous examples of the power of testimony. Consider the account in Mark 5 of the man whom Jesus delivered from a legion of demons:

> As Jesus was getting into the boat, the man who had been demon-possessed [possessed with a legion of demons] begged to go with him.[5]

The newly delivered man wanted to go with Jesus, but Jesus had another thought in mind. He said to the man, "Go home to your own people and tell them how much the Lord has done for you, and how he has had mercy on you."[6]

The story continues. The man went away into a region of ten cities—the Decapolis—and began to broadcast what Jesus had done for him. Regarding the impact of his testimony, the Bible reports, "And all the people were amazed."[7] His amazing transformation affected amazing results in the lives of others as he shared his story.

---

[5] Mark 5:18.

[6] Mark 5:19.

[7] Mark 5:20.

I also love the example found in the story of the woman healed from twelve years of bleeding. She said to herself, "If I could just touch his cloak, I will be healed."[8] The woman pressed through the crowd, came up behind Jesus and did just as she had purposed in her heart to do. She touched the edge of his cloak, and she was instantly healed![9] This miracle occurred in Matthew 9.

Between Matthew 9 and 14, something significant happened. Matthew 14:34-36 reads,

> When they had crossed over, they landed at Gennesaret. And when the men of that place recognized Jesus, they sent word to all the surrounding country. People brought all their sick to him and begged him to *let the sick just touch the edge of his cloak, and all who touched it were healed* [emphasis mine].[10]

Why were these people asking for the sick to be allowed to touch the edge of Jesus' cloak? They had heard the story of the woman who touched the edge of His cloak! They had heard what had been done before. How did they hear of what had been done before? In all likelihood, the woman had been sharing her testimony. She had been telling her story. Testifying is what the Holy Spirit does. Concerning the Holy Spirit, Jesus said, "He will testify about me."[11] Then He said, "You also must testify."[12] When you testify, you are partnering with the Holy Spirit.

There is more to the Holy Spirit's role in this matter of testifying. Before His ascension into heaven, Jesus said to His followers, "You will

---

[8] Matthew 9:21 (paraphrased).

[9] Matthew 9:20-22.

[10] Matthew 14:34-36.

[11] John 15:26.

[12] John 15:27.

receive power when the Holy Spirit comes on you, and you will be witnesses unto me."[13]

What does it mean to be "witnesses" unto Jesus? What is a witness? A witness is a person who has seen or heard something and then tells about it. Consider the account of Peter and John standing before the Sanhedrin in Acts 4. These two apostles said, "As for us, we cannot help speaking about what we have seen and heard."[14] As a witness, you have seen and heard some things, and now you live to tell about them.

Summary

In summary, remember that when you testify, you glorify God. You strengthen your own faith. You remind yourself of what God has done. You strengthen the faith of others. You deliver grace into the present situation and greatly increase the likelihood that God will do it again.

Using the space that follows this section, devote an hour or two to writing your testimony in three parts:

1. **My life before my encounter with Christ.** There is no need to go into great detail. Try not to overemphasize the darkness. Remember that this testimony is ultimately a testimony about how great God is and not a testimony about how bad the devil is or what a terrible sinner you were.

2. **My encounter with Christ.**[15] How did God set you up for this encounter? What actually happened? What changed on that day?

---

[13] Acts 1:8.

[14] Acts 4:20. See also 1 John 1:1-4.

[15] If you have not yet had a personal encounter with Christ, read the "Personal Spirituality" section in the chapter entitled, "Managing Yourself." There you will be given instructions for beginning your relationship with God through His Son, Jesus.

Your Story

3. **My life after my encounter with Christ.** What is different now? What new direction is your life taking? Tell this part of your story in a way that encourages others to trust God for a similar manifestation of grace in their life.

What is your testimony?

1. Describe your life before your encounter with Christ.

2. Describe your encounter with Christ.

3. Describe the life you are now living after your encounter with Christ.

Gateway to the Christian College Experience

Chapter 2
Your College

Your college has produced a number of documents and services to help you become acclimated to the college experience. During opening orientation, administrative personnel typically draw the attention of students to these items. Three essential documents are the Academic Catalog, the Student Handbook and the Syllabi for each course. In addition, typically the college's online Learning Management System provides a means for consolidating and simplifying many functions for the student. This chapter serves as an introduction to these key components.

Academic Catalog

Locate and open your college's Academic Catalog. Some colleges still provide hard copy editions of their catalog, while others only make it available digitally as either a downloadable document or as a section on the college website. Take time right now to locate the Academic Catalog; you will need it for many of the exercises that follow.

Your first task in this chapter is to tour your college by finding and reviewing the following items in your Academic Catalog:

1. Mission Statement
2. Vision Statement
3. Purpose Statement
4. Institutional Goals
5. Core Values
6. Faith Statement

7. History
8. Campus Facilities and Services
9. Graduation Requirements
10. Grading System
11. Attendance Policy
12. Change of Status Policies
13. Satisfactory Academic Progress
14. Academic Programs
15. Course Descriptions
16. Faculty and Administration

Mission Statement

Once you have located the Academic Catalog, go directly to the Table of Contents. Find the page where the Mission Statement is posted, and turn there.

Mission statements communicate *what* an institution or individual does to fulfill a calling or purpose. Before you review the college's mission statement, pause and reflect for a few moments on what you believe to be *your personal life-mission*. Pondering this question may assist in the discovery of your personal life-mission: "What will I do to fulfill my life's purpose and calling?" Even if you cannot definitively answer this question, take time to dream a bit. Complete this reflection assignment, and then review the college's mission statement.

What is your personal life-mission?

My mission in life is to…

Having reflected on what you believe to be your personal life-mission, carefully read the college's mission statement as it appears in the Academic Catalog. What parts of it are especially appealing to you? If you are reviewing a hard copy of the catalog, you may want to highlight or underline key words or phrases. If you are reviewing a digital version of the catalog on your electronic device, jot down a few notes on paper or in your notebook. Once you have written your preliminary thoughts, use those notes to help you complete the following exercise.

> **Note the parts of the college's mission statement that seem especially relevant to you. How does your personal life-mission align with the mission of this school?**

Vision Statement

A vision statement describes *where* an institution is going. It provides a prophetic picture of a desired destination. Locate and read the college's vision statement. If your college's catalog does not have a vision statement, then move on to the next section.

As you did with the mission statement, use the space that follows to note the parts of the vision statement that seem particularly important to you, and explain why you think those parts are relevant to your journey.

> **Note the parts of the college's vision statement that seem particularly important to you. Why are those parts relevant to your journey?**

Purpose Statement

In addition to mission and vision statements, some colleges also publish a statement of purpose. Locate and read your college's purpose statement. As you did with the mission statement, use the space below to note the parts of the purpose statement that seem particularly important to you, and explain why you think those parts are relevant to your journey. This exercise should help you to gain a stronger sense of purpose concerning why you have enrolled in this school.

What parts of the college's purpose statement seem especially relevant to you? Why?

Institutional Goals

Locate in the Academic Catalog the college's statement concerning its institutional goals or objectives. What parts of that statement seem particularly important to you? Why do you feel that way? Record your thoughts below.

What parts of the college's institutional goals or objectives seem especially relevant to you? Why?

Core Values

Core values comprise the substance of *why* an institution conducts itself a certain way. They are those non-negotiable principles that guide an organization and its constituents. When college leaders articulate core values, it is as though they are saying, "We *must* live by these values, if we are going to remain true to what God has called us to be and do."

Review your college's core values as presented in the Academic Catalog. As you have done with the previous items, use the space below to note the core values that align with your own ideals. Also note any values that may seem new to you. If your college has not published its core values, then you may skip this section, unless your professor instructs you otherwise.

Which core values align with your own ideals? Explain. Which core values seem new to you?

Gateway to the Christian College Experience

Faith Statement

You have enrolled in a Christian college that is guided by a belief system. Locate and review the college's statement of faith. As you did with the mission and purpose statements, use the space below to note the parts of the faith statement that resonate with your own beliefs. You may also want to note any articles of faith that may seem new to you.

Perhaps you have come from a faith background that is different from the faith culture of this school. Although your personal beliefs may be dissimilar in some ways, it is very important to become familiar with the doctrine of this institution. Even if you disagree with some minor point, it is important to at least honor that aspect of the college's faith while attending here.

After reviewing the faith statement, record your reflections below. What parts of the college's faith statement resonate with your own beliefs? What parts seem new to you?

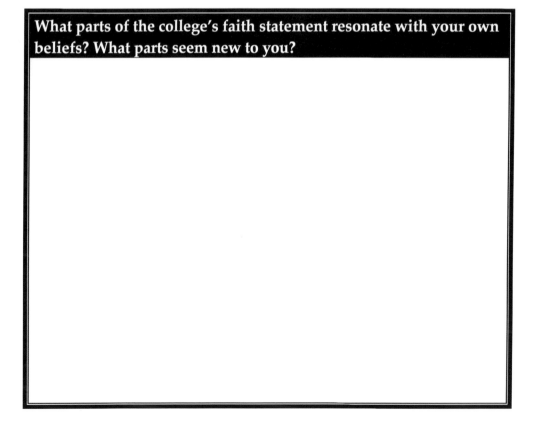

Your College

History

Locate and read the history of this college. When and where was this school founded? Who founded it? Why was it started? What about its history seems to still have a bearing on the way that it is currently functioning? What aspects of its history provide clues of where God might want to take this school in days to come? Record your thoughts below.

Basic Historical Facts

1. In what year was your school founded?

2. Where was it originally located?

3. Who founded the school?

4. Why was it started?

5. What about its history seems to still have a bearing on the way that it is currently functioning?

6. What aspects of the college's history provide clues of where God might want to take this school in days to come?

Campus Facilities and Services

Take time now to become familiar with the facilities and services that your college offers. Study the campus map. Become familiar with the names of the various buildings, and learn what takes place in each of those facilities.

Check off each of the following items as you locate them:

- ☐ Library
- ☐ Computer Lab
- ☐ Classrooms
- ☐ Lab Facilities
- ☐ Media Center / Studio
- ☐ Cafeteria
- ☐ Student Center
- ☐ Chapel
- ☐ Prayer Rooms / Center
- ☐ Bookstore

Your College

- ☐ Campus Post Office
- ☐ Administrative Offices:
  - ☐ Registrar's Office
  - ☐ Admissions Office
  - ☐ Enrollment Director's Office
  - ☐ Finance Office
  - ☐ Financial Aid Office
  - ☐ Campus Pastor's / Chaplain's Office
  - ☐ Student Life Office
  - ☐ Dean of Students' Office
  - ☐ Academic Affairs Office
  - ☐ President's Office
- ☐ Nurse's Office
- ☐ Faculty Offices
- ☐ Campus Security / Safety Office
- ☐ Sports Facilities
- ☐ Men's Dormitories
- ☐ Women's Dormitories
- ☐ Counseling Services
- ☐ Tutorial Services
- ☐ Learning and Writing Center

Graduation Requirements

You do not want to reach the final semester of your college experience only to discover that you had overlooked a graduation requirement. Here at the beginning of your journey, make sure that you are aware of all that it will take to qualify for graduation. Find the place in your Academic Catalog that addresses these concerns, and become familiar with those details.

Grading System

Be sure to find and review the grading scale that is published in the college's Academic Catalog. The syllabi for your courses will provide further details on how grades will be determined for each respective class that you are taking.

Attendance Policy

Check the Academic Catalog, the Student Handbook and each course syllabus for details concerning attendance policies. No matter what college you attend, you are expected to attend class. Unless classes are online or are facilitated as independent studies, typically you will need to be physically present in a specific place at a specific time. At the start of each semester, take note of the time and location for each class.

Being absent or tardy can negatively impact your performance and resulting grade in a course. If you are absent, you will inevitably miss content and processes essential to the course. Some colleges have an automatic fail policy that goes into effect after you have been absent a designated number of times. Missing class should be a rarity, but if you do miss, take responsibility for catching up or making up whatever you missed. Better yet, if you know in advance that you are going to miss, check-in with your professor to let him or her know.

In many Christian colleges, chapel attendance is also required. Some institutions even give a grade for chapel participation. Non-attendance in chapel services can result in adverse consequences, as far as grades are concerned.

Make yourself aware of all that your college expects from you as it relates to attendance. The best practice is to plan to be present for every required session and to reserve absences for absolute emergencies.

Online programs and independent / directed studies will have their own way of fulfilling the attendance requirement. Some online programs track attendance on the basis of engagement in discussion assignments. Independent / directed studies often count attendance on the basis of the student's participation in consultations with the professor. If you take an online course or enroll in an independent / directed study, become aware of how attendance requirements are met for those programs.

Change of Status Policies

Browse through your Academic Catalog to learn your college's policies pertaining to the following:

1. Withdrawing from a course
2. Withdrawing from the college
3. Adding a course
4. Changing your degree program
5. Requesting an incomplete for a course
6. Requesting an extension for coursework

You cannot just decide to stop attending a class without following the college's notification procedures. You must communicate with the Registrar's office, and follow prescribed procedures for withdrawing.

Similarly, you cannot just decide to pack up, quit college and go back home without telling the proper administrative authorities. You must follow the college's procedures for withdrawing from the school. If you fail to do so, you run the risk of facing major financial issues and possibly even legal issues as it relates to any Federal Student Aid, grants or scholarships that you have been awarded. Your transcript will also have an ugly scar on it that could haunt you for many years.

On a related issue, you cannot assume that professors will let you turn in late work after the course has concluded. You must follow the college's procedures for requesting either an incomplete or an extension. Making assumptions based on the perceived goodwill of your instructors is a dangerous thing to do.

Satisfactory Academic Progress

Find the place in the Academic Catalog that addresses Satisfactory Academic Progress (SAP). SAP relates to how you must continually perform academically in order to remain in college. Become fully aware of what you need to do in order to stay in school. The college will expect you to maintain a designated minimum Grade Point Average (GPA) from semester to semester. Students who do not satisfy SAP requirements run the risk of being suspended.

There are two GPA scores that you need to track throughout your college journey: your term GPA and your cumulative GPA. The term GPA is your Grade Point Average for a particular semester or term. Your cumulative GPA is calculated on the basis of *all* of your grades for *all* terms or semesters combined. Your college has a minimum term GPA, and it also has a minimum cumulative GPA that you must monitor. The minimum cumulative GPA that you must maintain typically increases as you advance in your academic program because it is based on the total number of credit hours that you have attempted.

What is the minimum term GPA that this college requires?	

What is the minimum cumulative GPA that this college requires at the time of your graduation? *Please remember that if you have not maintained the minimum cumulative GPA required for graduation, you will not be permitted to graduate.*	

As you progress through your academic journey, how does your college define what it requires for a minimum cumulative GPA? Your instructor may provide this information. If not, then look it up in the Satisfactory Academic Progress section located in either the Academic Catalog or in the Consumer Information posted on the college website.

Once you have located the information, enter it into the spaces provided in the table that follows.

After you have attempted...	You must have a cumulative GPA of...
1 - 29.5 semester hours	
30 - 44.5 semester hours	
45 – 59.5 semester hours	
60 – 74.5 semester hours	
75 -89.5 semester hours	
90 – 104.5 semester hours	

Academic Programs

One of the most common questions you will hear when people first meet you on campus is "What is your major?" While some students are very confident of their direction from the start, others are not yet sure what degree program they will pursue. Your academic advisor and others at the college are ready to help you think through your educational and career options.

Turn to the place in your Academic Catalog where academic / degree programs are described. It is a good idea to become generally familiar with this area of the catalog. Give particular attention to the specific academic program you have selected. If you are unsure and have not yet selected a specific academic program, complete this exercise on the basis of the program that appeals to you the most. Consult with your academic advisor for guidance in the selection of your degree program.

Locate your program (e.g., A.A.S. in Pastoral Studies or B.A. in Missions) and its description. Included with the description, you should also see a list of objectives or anticipated outcomes for your program. Typically the description and objectives will be followed by a list of the courses you will be taking in that program of study. Take time to read the description, and then carefully review the list of objectives or learning outcomes that the college wants you to achieve while enrolled in the program.

In the following exercise, you will write the name of your program (e.g., Associate of Applied Science in Pastoral Leadership, Bachelor of Arts in Intercultural Studies) and list the objectives that are stated in the Academic Catalog for that program. In the space provided beside each objective, record your personal reflections on how you believe that particular objective relates to you and what you hope to achieve in your college journey.

Your College

Your Academic Program

What is the name of your academic program?

_____

Objectives / Outcomes for this Program *as published in the Academic Catalog*	**Personal Reflections** *How do you believe each objective relates to what you hope to achieve in your college journey?*
Objective 1:	
Objective 2:	
Objective 3:	
Objective 4:	
Objective 5:	

Gateway to the Christian College Experience

Objective 6:	
Objective 7:	
Objective 8:	
Objective 9:	
Objective 10:	
Objective 11:	
Objective 12:	

After completing the previous exercise, review the list of courses that you will be taking in your program. Which of those courses are you taking this semester? Here you will need to refer to the course schedule that you received when you enrolled this semester. Taking time to complete the table below will help to make you aware of vital details pertaining to your classes.

Your Courses this Semester

Semester (e.g., fall, spring): _____ Year: _____

Course Number	Course Title	Credit Hours	Instructor	Day(s) of Week	Time	Room Number

Course Descriptions

Surveying the catalog's course descriptions will open your eyes to the opportunities within reach at your college. Becoming familiar with what these courses offer can actually help you to decide upon a degree program, if you have not already done so. Once you have received your list of courses for the semester, review the catalog descriptions for those classes to familiarize yourself with what to expect.

Faculty and Administration

Browse through the catalog pages where biographical profiles for college personnel are listed. Pay particular attention to the instructors who will be teaching your courses this semester. In addition to their credentials and degrees, take note of experiences that have qualified them for the courses that they teach. As you honor these men and women, you will increase the likelihood that you will personally benefit from the grace they carry in their lives.

Student Handbook

Students are required to become thoroughly familiar with the Student Handbook. The Handbook typically covers areas such as:

1. Behavioral and disciplinary policies,
2. Dress code,
3. Spiritual life,
4. Security and safety issues,
5. Emergency procedures,
6. Automobile and parking regulations,
7. Dormitory policies,
8. Student services,
9. Student life,
10. Student ministries,
11. Nondiscriminatory policies and
12. Academic integrity.

Syllabi

The word "syllabi" or "syllabuses" is the plural form of the singular word "syllabus." You will receive a syllabus for each course that you take. Each syllabus serves as an official statement of requirements and expectations pertaining to its respective course. Become thoroughly familiar with your syllabi. The content of course syllabi may vary from college to college and from course to course, but most will include the following features.

Course Title and Number

The course title and number on your syllabus will correspond to the title and number for the course as it appears in the Academic Catalog. Course numbers are alpha-numeric—they contain both letters and numbers. Letters in the course number help to group the course with others courses within the same discipline, and the numeric part helps to place the course in its proper place within a sequence of courses.

For instance, at Valor Christian College (Columbus, Ohio), for BIB101 Old Testament History, "101" indicates that it is an entry level course, and "BIB" indicates that it is a Bible course. In contrast, for BIB201 Life of Christ, "201" indicates that it is a more advanced course. For BIB301 Old Testament Intensive, at Valor Christian College, the fact that it is a three-hundred level course (301) indicates that it is an even more advanced Bible course designed for honors students. Become familiar with the significant aspects of course numbers at your college.

Course Description

The course description in the syllabus will match the description in the Academic Catalog. This synopsis gives the student a quick bird's eye view of what the course is all about.

Instructor's Contact Information and Office Hours

Take note of your instructor's contact information and office hours. Enter this information into your smart phone, your email directory and any other place where you record your important contacts.

As a matter of etiquette, it is generally best to schedule appointments with faculty members rather than just informally drop by their offices. Although most instructors do not mind an occasional spontaneous visit with a student, they prefer having the opportunity to prepare for that meeting—freeing that block of time from distractions to ensure that the student will have the instructor's undivided attention.

Learning Outcomes

The statement of course objectives or learning outcomes helps the student to clearly see what he or she can hope to know, be or do by the time the semester ends. Some colleges administer pre-tests at the start of courses to measure student knowledge against the stated outcomes. Toward the end of each course, they are given post-tests addressing the same outcomes to measure the degree to which academic progress has been achieved in those courses.

Reading Assignments

As soon as you receive a syllabus, take the following steps:

1. Purchase your own copy of every required textbook, and make sure you are acquiring the correct editions. Do not rely on using a library copy or borrowing a friend's copy. You need to be carrying that book with you frequently so that you can devour it at every available opportunity.
2. Note the dates in the course schedule when each reading assignment is to be completed. Record those assignments and dates on your personal calendar.
3. Become familiar with the titles listed under supplemental or suggested reading. When assignments call for writing papers, the list of supplemental texts may be a good place to begin research.

Writing Assignments

Review the syllabus thoroughly to become aware of every required writing assignment. Mark the due date for each assignment on your personal calendar, and then schedule for yourself week-by-week progress points throughout the semester leading up to the due date. Do not wait for the instructor to remind you about the writing assignment; take personal responsibility for it from the very beginning.

In addition to being aware of the scheduling of writing assignments, you also need to know detailed expectations pertaining to those papers. What style guide is required? How should it be formatted? Is the paper to be written formally or informally? Is it a reflection paper, or is it a research paper? How many pages are required? If it is a research paper, how many sources are required? These details may be supplied in the syllabus, but the instructor may choose to cover such guidelines in a class session. If you find yourself in doubt as to what is expected of you, be sure to ask.

Quizzes and Tests

Check the syllabus for the instructor's schedule and policy pertaining to quizzes and tests. Transfer quiz and test dates to your personal calendar, and be aware of the possibility that the instructor may occasionally give a "pop quiz" without previous notice.

Grading System

While the college may have a uniform grading system designed for use by all instructors in all courses, some courses might contain unique elements requiring a variation from the norm. Read each syllabus to become knowledgeable of each course's grading system.

Attendance and Participation Policies

While the intent of the college's participation policies is to generally cover most courses taught in the institution, some courses may have unusual components requiring variations from the norm. For instance, a performance-oriented class such as Preaching or Public Speaking would likely have a higher standard for classroom participation than a lecture-driven Systematic Theology class.

Be aware of posted attendance requirements, and track your own attendance on a weekly basis. College-level students should not need instructors to remind them that they have been absent. When you are absent from a class, you know that you are absent. Nonattendance leads to declining academic performance and poor grades.

Schedule

The schedule provides a sequential / chronological guide to course content and assignment due dates. At the start of the semester, transfer every date from the syllabus schedule to your personal calendar.

Bibliography

The bibliography represents a collection of resources deemed as significant influences toward the development of the course. Along with the list of required and supplemental readings, the bibliography serves as a helpful guide for the initiation of student research projects.

The Learning Management System

Most colleges require students to log onto and use their online Learning Management System (LMS). If you are already attending classes, at the start of the term, you should have been given access codes (username and password) for logging onto the LMS. If you have not yet received or have misplaced your access information, contact the LMS administrator or a school administrator (e.g., Registrar) immediately.

It is important to regularly access your professors' posts in the LMS. The system enables you to track assignments, grades, attendance and other aspects of class performance. For some schools, college announcements and email messages are also handled through the LMS.

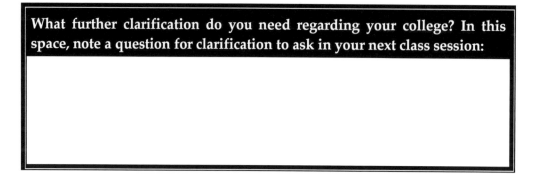

Chapter 3
Your Calling

You have a purpose in life, and God wants you to know that purpose. In fact, He delights in revealing that purpose to you. The communication of God's purpose and direction for a person's life is often referred to as a "calling."

The first and primary call upon your life is the call to follow Jesus. The Gospels report a number of occasions when He called followers with the words, "Follow me":

Matthew 4:19
"Come, follow me," Jesus said, "and I will send you out to fish for people."

Mark 10:21
Jesus looked at him [the rich young ruler] and loved him. "One thing you lack," he said. "Go, sell everything you have and give to the poor, and you will have treasure in heaven. Then come, follow me."[16]

Luke 5:27
After this, Jesus went out and saw a tax collector by the name of Levi sitting at his tax booth. "Follow me," Jesus said to him,

John 1:43
The next day Jesus decided to leave for Galilee. Finding Philip, he said to him, "Follow me."

John 21:19
Jesus said this to indicate the kind of death by which Peter would glorify God. Then he said to him [Peter], "Follow me!"

---

[16] This story is also told in Luke 18:22.

The call to follow Jesus is indeed a call to learn His teachings and to emulate His example. However, when Jesus called His first disciples, that call was not just a figurative gesture. It was a literal summons for them to *be* with Him—to constantly accompany Him.

Mark 3:13-15
Jesus went up on a mountainside and called to him those he wanted, and they came to him. He appointed twelve that they might be with him and that he might send them out to preach and to have authority to drive out demons.

Before Jesus could entrust the work of the kingdom to His disciples—preaching the Gospel and driving out demons, He first knew that they needed to spend quality time with Him. He wanted them to *know* Him. He wanted them to know His heart. They need more than instructions; they needed the spiritual and emotional impartation that could only come from being constantly in His company.

What is the point? The call of Jesus is first a call to spiritual intimacy. Before you concern yourself too much with what career you are going to pursue or what ministry endeavor you are going to take on, heed Jesus' call to draw close to Him—to know His heart. Doing so will ensure that your ministry or career will be carried the way that Jesus would do it.

Vocation

When I was a young boy I would hear people talk about "the call of God." Most often that expression was a reference to God's call upon a person's life to preach, to pastor, to evangelize or to serve as a missionary. Certainly we should respect those callings, but are they the only vocations to which the Lord calls people?

Even the word "vocation" suggests that the concept of "calling" encompasses much more. In its most elemental sense, the word "vocation" means "calling." The similarity between the first part of the word, "vocation," and the word, "vocal," provides a hint toward that fact. In generations past, it was believed that a person's sense of being drawn toward a particular field of labor or service was actually a call from God. Some may be called to be business leaders or educators. Others may be called to be artisans or physicians. Still others may be called to serve in church leadership. Once a person entered into their vocation, they were then to perform their duties for the glory of God.

Seven Mountains of Influence

In recent times, the church has returned to embracing the broader understanding of God's call. In the 1970's, Bill Bright, founder of Campus Crusade for Christ, and Loren Cunningham, founder of Youth With a Mission, got together and discovered that God had given both of them similar insights into how the mission of Christ was to impact culture and society. From what the Lord had shown them, God desired to extend his kingdom through seven mountains or spheres of influence:

1. Arts and Entertainment
2. Business and Science
3. Education
4. Family
5. Government
6. Media
7. Religion

> **Which of the seven mountains of influence seem especially appealing to you? Why?**

With sincere desire to please God, at times I have heard people make statements such as these:

> "I was in the corporate business world, but then I felt the call of God on my life, so I had to leave it to go into the ministry."

> "I have such a desire to be an educator, but I also feel God's call on my life. I'm not quite sure what I am to do."

God does occasionally call people out of other careers to place them in church work. However, one should not assume that God's call always means that a person is to leave their secular field. He needs people who will serve and represent Him powerfully and with intentionality in every sector of society. Thankfully God does still call people to serve Him in church ministry, but some who are reading this text should consider the possibility that His call may be for one of the other mountains of influence. Perhaps you should glorify Him in the area for which you are already passionate. Sure, the Lord may have something different in mind for you, but are you sure?

Recognizing God's Call

The recognition of God's call is a matter of knowing His voice. How can people know when God is truly speaking to them? How can one distinguish authentic revelation from mere imagination? Let us first consider the several ways in which God communicates, and then we will address how we can develop the ability to listen and hear what He has to say.

How God Speaks

How does God speak? There are a number of means that the Lord uses to reveal His heart, mind and purpose:

Creation. Romans 1:20 indicates that God communicates His invisible qualities through creation. Psalm 19:1-4 says that the heavens and skies proclaim God's glory and His works. Believers can easily relate to this truth. Who among us has not looked up into the starry skies on a cloudless night and thought, "How marvelous are your

Your Calling

works, God!" Yet, while He does speak of His existence through creation, that message is not heard and understood by all. Natural revelation alone does not sufficiently communicate all that the Creator has to say.

When decision-making becomes confused in the clutter of conflicting opinions, sometimes getting close to nature helps to bring internal clarity to the matter. If you live near an ocean or a lake, take a walk along the shoreline while communing with Jesus. Throw a blanket on the ground, lie back, and let your eyes follow the cloud formations as they float across the sky. Try the same thing at night. Survey the stars and planets; then allow your imagination to take you back in time to the moment when the Creator made it all. Gaze into the eyes of a newborn baby, and contemplate the wonders of God. Where does all of this reflecting take your thoughts concerning God and His purposes for your life? Pay attention to your thoughts, because some of them may actually be the very thoughts of God.

Scripture. 2 Timothy 3:16 says that all Scripture is inspired—"God-breathed." Long ago God spoke prophetically to holy men, they recorded what He said, and that record has been preserved for our benefit in the pages of the Bible. The Bible is the objective word of God. Other forms of divine communication are subject to that objective word—the Holy Scriptures. It is important to uphold Scripture as the standard by which all other forms of revelation are assessed. God will not speak in a way that conflicts with what He has already revealed in the Bible. He will not contradict Himself.

Set apart an hour, and immerse yourself in the pages of your Bible. Read it out loud. Read it slowly. Ponder each word until something leaps off of the page and into your heart. When that happens, stop right there. God is talking to you! Listen. Respond to Him. Continue the conversation. Then when it is all over, open your journal and write down what He has said.[17]

---

[17] This approach to Bible reading is a devotional method. It should not be regarded as a substitute for the careful study of Scripture.

Prophetic Guidance. In light of 1 Corinthians 12-14, we know that the Holy Spirit guides us through words of knowledge, words of wisdom and the discerning of spirits. This kind of guidance can come internally as the Spirit speaks to us directly, or it can come through other people as they speak to us from the heart of God. Supernatural guidance can also come through dreams, visions and angelic visitations. Prophetic guidance is a subjective form of guidance and should be tested in light of Scripture. Typically a safe rule of thumb is to receive any prophetic word from another person as a *potential* word from God. It is up to you to discern whether or not it is truly God speaking.

Wise Counsel. Who are the people that seem to always show up in your life whenever you need guidance? Who are the people whose advice most often turns out to be right? Who are the people who have proven to be a consistent source of wisdom in your life? Learn to seek out these people. Listen to them, and carefully weigh what they have to say.

How can a person be sure that the wisdom offered by others is truly wisdom from God? James 3 offers a good guideline:

> The wisdom that comes from heaven is first of all pure; then peace-loving, considerate, submissive, full of mercy and good fruit, impartial, and sincere.[18]

Based on the words of James, these questions should be asked regarding any particular proposed word of advice:

1. Does it promote purity?
2. Is it peace-loving?
3. Is it considerate of others?
4. Does it promote submission to authority?
5. Is it full of mercy?
6. Does it reflect the goodness of God, and does it have the potential for producing good fruit?

---

[18] James 3:17.

7. Is it impartial?
8. Is it sincere, promoting honesty and truthfulness?

Personal Desires. Philippians 2:13 says that "it is God who works in you to will and to act in order to fulfill his good purpose." For the person who walks closely with God, their desires will be His desires. Often that which a devoted Christian desires can be one of several indicators of God's will in a situation.

When people walk intimately with God, they *can* often know God's will intuitively. Without having to do much analysis, the way is clear. One direction feels right while another feels wrong. Intuition is a subjective form of guidance and should be tested in light of Scripture.

Circumstantial Confirmations. There are times when God in His sovereignty aligns circumstances and brings key people into our lives to confirm His will and guidance. Often the Lord has already been speaking to us in other ways when such alignment and confirmation takes place.

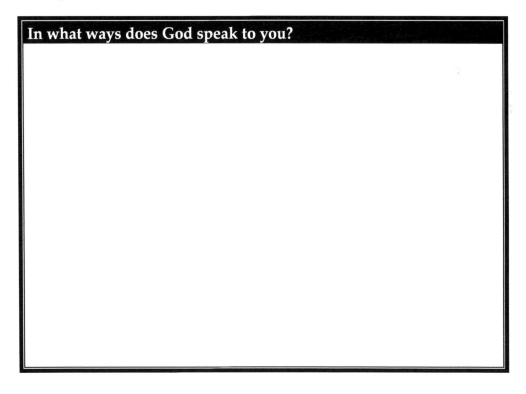

In what ways does God speak to you?

Developing the Ability to Hear

We can develop the ability to hear God's voice. An earnest desire to hear Him is a good place to start. I am always inspired by the story of the woman named Mary who was captivated by Jesus and sat at His feet with a yearning to hear everything He has to say:

> **Luke 10:38-42**
> As Jesus and his disciples were on their way, he came to a village where a woman named Martha opened her home to him. She had a sister called Mary, who sat at the Lord's feet listening to what he said. But Martha was distracted by all the preparations that had to be made. She came to him and asked, "Lord, don't you care that my sister has left me to do the work by myself? Tell her to help me!"
>
> "Martha, Martha," the Lord answered, "you are worried and upset about many things, but few things are needed—or indeed only one. Mary has chosen what is better, and it will not be taken away from her."

Like Mary's sister, Martha, there are those who feel that the Christian life is all about working for God. Yes, there is work to be done, but Jesus is more concerned about having a relationship of love and friendship with His followers. He is hoping that we will all be like Mary, who loved Him so much that she could not get enough of listening to what He had to say.

Our very life depends on hearing and heeding the voice of God. When Jesus was tempted by the devil to turn stones into bread, Jesus said, "It is written, 'Man does not live on bread alone, but on every word that comes from the mouth of God.'"[19]

What lesson can we learn from these words? A spiritual life cannot be sustained by natural means. A spiritual life can only be sustained by "every word that comes from the mouth of God." When Jesus said, "every word that comes from the mouth of God," He was not just talking about Scripture as God's Word. He meant everything that God

---

[19] Matthew 4:4.

Your Calling

has to say, whatever way He may choose to say it—whether it be through the Bible or some other means.

Cultivate a hunger for this kind of bread—"every word that comes from the mouth of God." Stir up a hunger for the sound of His voice. Have an attitude that says, "I can't wait to hear the next thing that He has to say. I can't wait to take the next thing that He says, devour it, embrace it, integrate it into my life, and act upon it."

Our effectiveness in our mission depends on hearing and heeding the voice of God. We must follow the example of Jesus, when He said,

> **John 5:19**
> "The Son can do nothing of his own accord, but only what he sees the Father doing; for whatever he does, that the Son does likewise."

If Jesus had to rely upon His Father's guidance for everything that He did, how much more should we rely upon divine guidance. Try exercising this practice of discerning what the Father is doing. The next time you are sitting in a restaurant or walking across campus, quietly say to God, "What are you doing right now? I want to do what you are doing. I want to align my thoughts, words and actions with yours." This practice is an important part of training yourself to discern the voice of God.

Expect to hear the Lord's voice. There are a number of Bible passages that should elevate our expectation that God is ready to speak to us:

> **John 10:27**
> My sheep listen to my voice; I know them, and they follow me.

> **Isaiah 30:21**
> Thine ears shall hear a word behind thee, saying, This is the way, walk ye in it, when ye turn to the right hand, and when ye turn to the left.

> **Isaiah 50:4**
> The Sovereign Lord has given me a well-instructed tongue, to know the word that sustains the weary. He wakens me morning by morning, wakens my ear to listen like one being instructed.

John 16:13
When he, the Spirit of truth, is come, he will guide you into all truth.

We can grow in our ability to hear. Jesus gave us a few keys for developing our ability to hear when He said,

Mark 4:24
"Consider carefully what you hear," he continued. "With the measure you use, it will be measured to you—and even more."

What can we learn from these words? God will measure to us "even more" revelation, if we will come to Him with the intent to "consider carefully" whatever He has to say to us. He also wants us to consider the size of the scoop—or measure—we are using to receive His words. In other words, how much are we expecting to receive? If we expect to receive a thimble full of revelation, that is how much we will receive, plus a little more. If we expect to fill a tanker truck with revelation, that is how much we will receive, plus a good deal more.

Simply stated, our ability to hear God's voice will increase when we do the following:

1. Place a high value on the sound of His voice—His Word. Refuse to live your life without that sound.

2. Listen with the intent of carefully considering whatever He says. Before you even hear His voice, make the decision: "I am going to believe whatever He says. I am going to take it to heart. I am going to obey His instructions. I am going to live by what He says." When we are faithful with a little, He will trust us with more.[20]

3. Listen with great expectation. Approach Him with a huge measure. The Lord will meet you to the level of your expectation, and then He will do something beyond that expectation simply because He loves you and wants to.

---

[20] Luke 16:10.

Your Calling

How do *you* plan to develop your ability to hear God's voice?

Describe what you believe to be God's call on your life. If you do not know for sure, describe what you might *hope* to be God's call on your life.

God's call anticipates an answer. Write a prayer to your heavenly Father in response to His call.

Chapter 4
Your Goals and Plans

Having considered your calling, now identify what you think you will need for fulfilling that calling while you are attending this college. Once you have identified what you need, then you will set a few goals. Then after you have set goals, you will develop a plan for reaching each of those goals.

Your Needs

Turn back to the previous chapter, and think about your calling. What are the things standing in the way of you fulfilling your calling? What do you need? What training do you need? What resources do you need? Are there people who should be brought alongside you to help you fulfill your dreams? Are you in need of specific opportunities? What else do you need for this journey?

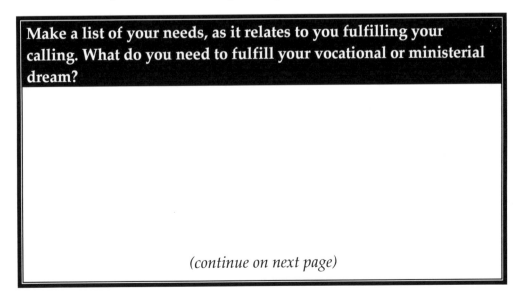

Make a list of your needs, as it relates to you fulfilling your calling. What do you need to fulfill your vocational or ministerial dream?

(continue on next page)

(continued from previous page)

Your Goals

As you think about the needs you have just noted, consider what goals should be set for addressing those needs. Think of goals that might be attainable while attending this college. Do your best to correlate your goals with specific needs.

In the space provided below, write three goals. Make sure that they are specific and measureable goals. Make sure they are goals you can realistically pursue while in college. Give yourself a deadline for each of your goals.

Example #1: My goal is to finish college debt free.

Example #2: My goal is to become a confident preacher by the end of my second year.

Example #3: My goal is to write my personal business plan before I graduate.

In light of your calling and your developmental needs, what three goals do you want to reach while attending this college?

1.

2.

(continue on next page)

> *(continued from previous page)*
>
> **3.**

Now that you have written down your goals, go back and circle the one that is most important to you. That goal is the one to which you may need to give the greatest focus during your time in this college.

Your Plans

On the following pages, you will draft a plan for each of the three goals you have set. Each planning sheet provides a place to rewrite the goal followed by spaces for writing a three-step plan. You will note resources, opportunities and partners needed for fulfilling your plan. When thinking about needed partners, consider individuals who will hold you accountable to following through with your plans. Finally you will state how you will know that you have reached the goal and what you expect the outcome or impact of your plan to be.

When you are finished, stop and pray over the plans you have made. Ask God for empowering grace for each step. After the three planning sheets, you will find a progress report page. As you advance through your school program, use that page to track progress toward reaching your goals. Each time you make note of an accomplishment, let it become an opportunity to give thanks to God.

Your Goals and Plans

Plan #1

Goal:

My Three-Step Plan:

    Step 1:

    Step 2:

    Step 3:

Resources, Opportunities and Partners I will need:

How I will know I have reached my goal:

What the anticipated outcome / impact will be:

Plan #2

Goal:

My Three-Step Plan:

    Step 1:

    Step 2:

    Step 3:

Resources, Opportunities and Partners I will need:

How I will know I have reached my goal:

What the anticipated outcome / impact will be:

Plan #3

Goal:

My Three-Step Plan:

Step 1:

Step 2:

Step 3:

Resources, Opportunities and Partners I will need:

How I will know I have reached my goal:

What the anticipated outcome / impact will be:

Gateway to the Christian College Experience

Progress Report			
Date	Progress toward Goal #1	Progress toward Goal #2	Progress toward Goal #3

Chapter 5
Attitudes for Success

When I was a child struggling to learn some new task, I remember on a few occasions muttering to my father, "But I can't." Dad's response was firm, yet kind: "There is no such word as 'can't.'" My father, Jim Turpin, instilled in me an attitude that would allow no room for defeat. He taught me to think in terms of success, and that is the mindset I aim to cultivate in this chapter.

Steve Backlund of Bethel Church in Redding, California, refers to such attitudes as "victorious mindsets." Steve is famous for saying, "Every area of your life not glistening with hope is under the influence of a lie."[21] It is important to identify the lies we believe and to counter those lies with truth.

Be careful to *not* believe the internal lies that sometimes bombard the minds of college students—lies such as these:

> "Success in college mostly depends on how a person performed in academics prior to coming here. I did not perform well before, and I'll not likely perform well now."

> "Some people have what it takes to succeed, and others don't. I don't."

> "I am here for the spiritual part of Christian college and not so much for the academic part."

---

[21] Steve Backlund notes that he learned this concept from Francis Frangipane. Steve Backlund, "Renewing the Mind," Igniting Hope Ministries, last modified 2015, accessed August 8, 2015, http:// ignitinghope.com/renewing-the-mind/. See also Romans 15:13 and Hebrews 10:23.

"Most of the other students in this college have everything going for them. Not me."

"I'm stupid."

"No one really wants to be around me."

"There is no way that I can get an 'A' in this course."

These statements are so far from the truth that they are laughable.[22] Thoughts such as these do not come from the heart and mind of God. If God is not thinking these kinds of thoughts concerning you, you should not be thinking these kinds of thoughts concerning you either.

The Power of Your Words

If you want to know the direction a person's life is taking, just listen to the way they talk. The Bible speaks of the tongue as being like a small rudder that steers the direction of a ship.[23] Words that we speak determine the direction of our life. When people declare a thing, they increase the likelihood that it will happen. That principle can have a positive or negative impact on a person's life, depending on whether a person's words are positive or negative. When you make a declaration of a desired outcome based on God's truth, you increase the likelihood that the truth you have spoken will be manifested in your life.

Spiritual dynamics are at play when we speak. Things that we say can actually affect the activities of spiritual forces and entities. However, even if nothing spiritual were at work, words still affect outcomes. When a person speaks a thing, the brain immediately goes to work to make arrangements for that thing to be fulfilled. Once again, this principle can work both positively and negatively.

---

[22] In my Success in College class at Valor Christian College, I read these "lies" aloud to the class, and after reading each lie, I say, "Let's laugh at that!" Then the class laughs at the lie, as a faith action to break its power off of their minds.

[23] James 3:4-5a.

Our words and our thoughts are important because they affect our whole being. The good news is that negative mindsets can be transformed into positive mindsets whenever people decide to intentionally renew their minds. The Bible says that we are to "be transformed by the renewing of our minds."[24]

To intentionally renew the mind, one must take negative thoughts captive. The Bible says, "We take captive every thought to make it obedient to Christ."[25] Catch that thought the moment that it shows up in your brain, and say, "You don't belong here! Get out!" Then replace that lie with truth by declaring the truth.

Personalized Declarations

One of the most powerful Bible reading exercises is to personalize verses of Scripture, converting them into prayers or declarations. A few examples have been provided below, demonstrating how to compose personalized declarations of truth. Read each of the noted verses, and then speak the corresponding declaration. Afterwards, open your Bible and locate some of God's promises that you have already underscored or highlighted. Practice converting those promises into declarations, and speak them aloud.

> **1 John 5:4**
> "Everyone born of God overcomes the world. This is the victory that has overcome the world, even our faith."
>
> **Declaration:** "I am born of God, and I am overcoming the world. My life originates from Him. The world cannot defeat me."

---

[24] Romans 12:2.

[25] 2 Corinthians 10:5.

Romans 8:37
"No, in all these things we are more than conquerors through him who loved us."

> **Declaration:** "I am more than a conqueror through Jesus, and He loves me."

Isaiah 41:10
"So do not fear, for I am with you;
  do not be dismayed, for I am your God.
I will strengthen you and help you;
  I will uphold you with my righteous right hand."

> **Declaration:** "I am not afraid. God is with me. I refuse to be discouraged. He is my God. He strengthens me. He helps me. He upholds me with His righteous right hand."

Philippians 2:13
"For it is God who works in you to will and to act in order to fulfill his good purpose."

> **Declaration:** "God has created in me the desire to do His will. My decisions are wise. My actions are powerful. My desires are pleasing to God and fulfill His good purpose."

Romans 6:14
"For sin shall no longer be your master, because you are not under the law, but under grace."

> **Declaration:** "Sin is not my master. I am ruled by grace."

Philippians 4:19
"And my God will meet all your needs according to the riches of his glory in Christ Jesus."

> **Declaration:** "My God meets all my needs according to the riches of His glory in Christ Jesus."

Romans 12:2
"Do not conform to the pattern of this world, but be transformed by the renewing of your mind. Then you will be able to test and approve what God's will is—his good, pleasing and perfect will."

> **Declaration:** "The world does not shape my life. My mind is being renewed, and my renewed mind is transforming my life. With a renewed mind, I test and approve what God's will is. With a renewed mind, I know what He desires of me. His will is good. His will is pleasing. His will is perfect."

1 Corinthians 6:19
"Do you not know that your bodies are temples of the Holy Spirit, who is in you, whom you have received from God? You are not your own."

> **Declaration:** "My body is a temple—a holy dwelling for the Holy Spirit. He lives in me. I am not my own. I belong to Him."

1 Peter 5:7
"Cast all your anxiety on him because he cares for you."

> **Declaration:** "I cast all of my worries and fears on Jesus. He cares for me."

Matthew 28:20
"[Teach] them to obey everything I have commanded you. And surely I am with you always, to the very end of the age."

> **Declaration (directed to Jesus):** "I will do everything you command me."
>
> **Declaration:** "Jesus is always with me."

Galatians 6:9
"Let us not become weary in doing good, for at the proper time we will reap a harvest if we do not give up."

> **Declaration:** "I will not become weary of doing good works. I *will* reap a harvest. I will not give up."

John 10:10
"The thief comes only to steal and kill and destroy; I have come that they may have life, and have it to the full."

> **Declaration:** "The devil may try to steal from me, kill me and destroy me, but he will not prevail. Jesus came to give me life. I have that life, and it is a *full* life."

> **John 5:19**
> "Jesus gave them this answer: 'Very truly I tell you, the Son can do nothing by himself; he can do only what he sees his Father doing, because whatever the Father does the Son also does.'"
>
> **Declaration:** "I can do nothing of eternal worth by myself. I watch for what my Father is doing. Then I align my actions with His. Whatever the Father does, that is what I want to do."
>
> **Declaration (directed to the Father):** "Father, where you go, I go. What you say, I say. What you do, I do."

Now it is your turn. On the basis of the following verses from the Bible, write your own declarations.

> **2 Timothy 1:7**
> "For the Spirit God gave us does not make us timid, but gives us power, love and self-discipline."
>
> **Declaration:**

2 Timothy 2:15
"Do your best to present yourself to God as one approved, a worker who does not need to be ashamed and who correctly handles the word of truth."

Declaration:

Colossians 3:1-2
"Since, then, you have been raised with Christ, set your hearts on things above, where Christ is, seated at the right hand of God. Set your minds on things above, not on earthly things."

Declaration:

Attitudes for Success

2 Corinthians 10:3-5
"For though we live in the world, we do not wage war as the world does. The weapons we fight with are not the weapons of the world. On the contrary, they have divine power to demolish strongholds. We demolish arguments and every pretension that sets itself up against the knowledge of God, and we take captive every thought to make it obedient to Christ."

Declaration:

Philippians 4:8
"Finally, brothers and sisters, whatever is true, whatever is noble, whatever is right, whatever is pure, whatever is lovely, whatever is admirable—if anything is excellent or praiseworthy—think about such things."

Declaration:

Be aware that with your attitude, actions and words, you have the power to change your environment and shift the atmosphere around you. Collective mindsets of others affect us more than we realize. You can walk into a room of negative thinking people and feel it. Likewise, you can walk into a room of positively thinking people and feel it. With one word spoken in faith, you can shift the atmosphere. You can make a difference in the mental and emotional orientation of the people around you.

Core Values

Whether we are aware of it or not, we all live by a set of core values. What are core values? Core values are the guiding principles of our life. They represent the things that are most important to us. For some people, things like "fun" or "friendship" may be core values. For others, "success" and "security" may be core values. Still others may say that "honesty" and "sincerity" are the key principles that guide their lives.

Followers of Jesus typically discover that they are guided by a set of core values that are very different from those of non-believers. Take a few moments to consider the values listed below. Do any of them reflect the way you would like to conduct your life while attending this college? Place a check mark beside any that seem relevant to you.

> **Which of these values reflect the way you would like to conduct your life while attending this college?**
>
> ☐   1.   Jesus as your focus and model for life and ministry
>
> ☐   3.   The Bible as the authoritative guide for your life
>
> ☐   4.   The goodness of God
>
> ☐   5.   Identity based upon a correct understanding of the Gospel
>
> ☐   6.   Honor: celebrating who people are without stumbling over what they are not[26]

☐ 7. Community: doing life together as "family"

☐ 8. Worship and prayer

☐ 9. Freedom coupled with responsibility

☐ 10. Stewardship of God's presence

☐ 11. Purity and integrity

☐ 12. Power: Spirit-empowered life and ministry

☐ 13. The prophetic

☐ 14. Faith as risk

☐ 15. Hope

☐ 16. Love: the essential ingredient of excellence

☐ 17. Mission: the advancement of God's kingdom through every believer and in every sector of society

Revisiting Your College's Core Values

Obviously colleges have rules for governing student conduct. While abiding by *rules* is important, conducting yourself in harmony with the institution's *core values* is of greater benefit toward your development as a person. Rules change from one environment to another, but core values established in the light of God's Word have the potential to stay with you for a lifetime. Go back to chapter two and review the core values that you noted from your college's Academic Catalog or Student Handbook.

Defining Your Personal Core Values

What are *your* core values? Take some time to think about it. You may want to adopt some of the aforementioned values; however, do not feel that you have to be limited to those. Using the space provided on the next page, make a list of at least seven core values that seem especially important to you during this season of your life.

Your Core Values

Chapter 6
Managing Yourself

Many college students are young adults who have not yet had a great deal of experience in managing their own lives. Previously there were other adults in their lives who provided the boundaries and told them what to do. Although institutions of higher education do define boundaries and expectations, generally speaking, college students must manage their own lives. In this chapter we will consider several specific areas of life management.

Time

Years ago I heard international evangelist Carl Richardson say, "You have something the Queen of England has!" What is it? After a pause, he said, "You have twenty-four hours in a day!"

Everybody has exactly the same amount of time. If everyone has the same amount of time, why do some people accomplish so much more than others? What differs from person to person is the way that they steward that time.

Priorities

I once asked a successful denominational leader how he was able to accomplish so much. He answered, "On the day of my arrival in this job, I was already behind in my work. On the day that I leave this job, I will be behind in my work. The key to success is prioritizing what I do between those two points in time."

How can a person effectively prioritize the multitude of tasks and responsibilities that cry out for attention? Perhaps the following suggestions will help:

1. Give priority to matters of eternal importance. Ask yourself, "Which of these tasks or responsibilities have the potential to make a difference that will really matter ten thousand years from now?"

2. Give priority to things that will improve the quality of life for *someone else*.

3. Give priority to things that will improve the quality of *your* life.

4. Give priority to those things that only you can do. For instance, only I can be a husband to my wife. Only I can be a son to my father. Only I can be a father to my daughter. Only I can improve the quality of my relationship with God. Someone else can do a lot of the other things, but there are some things that only I can do.

5. Give priority attention to people and secondary attention to things. Try to be more people-oriented than task-oriented. When I apply this principle to office work, I say it this way: "People over paper." In other words, the people around me are more important than all of the paperwork. The paperwork must still be completed, but if I will first invest in people, they will become empowered to do much of the work that otherwise might unnecessarily fall back to me.

6. Give priority attention to preparation and planning. Taking care in these areas will ultimately make you more productive.

One way to prioritize tasks, responsibilities and projects flows from the acronym, D.E.A.R., a slight modification of author Timothy Ferriss' D.E.A.L.[26]

1. **Define.** *Define* your life-mission. What do you want to accomplish in life? Write it down. *Define* your goals. What destinations do you need to reach in life in order to accomplish your life-mission? Write them down. *Define* your plans. What steps do you need to take in order to reach each of those goals? Write it all down. *Define* the one step that you will take today toward one of your goals. *Define* the one step that you will take within the next six hours toward that goal.

---

[26] Timothy Ferriss, *The 4-Hour Workweek* (New York: Harmony Books, 2009). In Ferriss' book, "D.E.A.L." stands for "Define," "Eliminate," "Automate" and "Liberate."

For example, for a number of years I have lived by a clear definition of my mission. My *life-mission* is to partner with God for the spiritual awakening of America. I live for the purpose of empowering the rising generation of leaders to ignite fires of revival in every conceivable sphere of influence. My *goals* and *plans* for fulfilling that mission involve praying, preaching, teaching, mentoring, writing books and shaping curriculum in ministry training settings. Each of those items could be broken down into detailed steps defining when, where and how they will be accomplished.

2. **Eliminate.** *Eliminate* everything from your life that does not advance the mission, goals and plans that you have defined. *Eliminate* from today anything that does not contribute to these purposes. If this elimination process causes you to worry that something important might be removed from your life, then you may need to revisit and revise your mission and goals.

3. **Automate.** *Automate* reoccurring tasks. Develop systems for handling routines so you do not have to reinvent procedures every time you face similar situations.

4. **Release.** You do not always have to do everything yourself. Empower others to assist with the project at hand. There are usually parts of any project that you can *release* for others to perform.

The "release" component of this model may not be as applicable to your college work as it will be in your career beyond college. Outsourcing should never become a method for avoiding responsibilities that only you should be fulfilling.

Calendar

Maintain a calendar. Go through the syllabi for your courses, note the due dates, and enter them into your calendar. Once you have identified due dates, think through how long it will take you to complete those projects.

Schedule a series of checkpoints on your calendar leading up to each due date. For instance, for a paper due on December 1, the following schedule of checkpoints might be helpful:

1. September 1: Finalize topic selection
2. September 15: Complete bibliography
3. October 1: Complete research
4. October 15: Complete outline
5. November 1: Compose first draft
6. November 15: Compose final draft
7. December 1: Submit final paper

Task Lists

Toward the end of your work day, make a list of the tasks for the following day. One way to prioritize a task list is to divide those items according to the following categories:

1. **Must:** What I *must* do.
2. **Should:** What I *should* do.
3. **Want:** What I *want* to do.

Ideally a person should accomplish something out of all three categories each day. It is true that your time at college may require you to devote most of your energies to the "must" and "should" categories; however, often movement toward fulfilling your dreams and passions is accomplished by going after a few things that you *want* to do.

On the following page you will find a daily planning sheet that divides your tasks into the "must," "should" and "want" categories. Make a few photocopies of the planning sheet, and try your hand at using it to plan what you hope to accomplish tomorrow. The planning sheet is on the next page.

Managing Yourself

Daily Planning Sheet

Date:

Must	Should

Want

Learning to Say "No"

Going to college can be like going to Disney World or Six Flags. At a theme park, you want to ride all the rides and see all the attractions. You are likely to think, "I don't want to miss anything!" Similarly, at this college you will be introduced to numerous extracurricular activities that will place demands on your time (e.g., social events, ministry outreaches, community service projects). It may appear that all of these opportunities are worthy of your time; however, you do not have to do everything in your first month or even your first semester of college. Remember that you have two to four years (depending on the length of your degree program) to participate in the Christian college experience. Learn to prioritize and schedule your activities. Practice saying "no" or "maybe another time" whenever necessary.

Money

Life management includes money management. Tell your money what to do. Do not let your money tell you what to do. Just because you still have $50 in your checking account doesn't necessarily mean that you can now go out to eat with your friends. If that $50 checkbook balance is whispering to you, "Go ahead. Go out to eat," then you are letting your money tell you what to do.

What obligations will you have a week from now or two weeks from now? Will you need that $50 at that time? When will additional funds be deposited into your account? You have got to think through questions such as these.

Budgeting

How does a person tell their money what to do? When you prepare a written budget, you are telling your money what to do. How much money will you be receiving as income each month? Calculate the total of your revenue streams. How much money will you be spending each month? Add it all up. If the amount you will be spending exceeds the amount of your income, then you need to either increase your income or reduce your expenses. If spending is less than income, then place the difference in savings. Better yet, regular contributions to a savings account should be included in the expenditure column of your budget. Your budget should be balanced; the total of your income column should equal the total of your expenditure column.

When preparing your budget, learn to distinguish between non-discretionary and discretionary spending. Non-discretionary spending is spending required by a contract or commitment you have made. If you have a car payment, that obligation is a non-discretionary expense. You *must* make that car payment, and it is for a specific amount that you can anticipate from month to month. If you have made a commitment to return to the Lord a tithe (ten percent) of your income, that tithe is a non-discretionary expenditure.

Discretionary spending includes more flexible items such as groceries, clothing and entertainment. You can choose at your own discretion whether to buy those new sneakers now or to postpone that purchase until a later time. You have the liberty to be selective about the purchase of grocery items. You can decide to either see that new movie in the theatre or to wait until you can rent the DVD when it comes out. Do not use money designated for non-discretionary expenses for discretionary items.

Paying for College

While in college, paying for your education must remain one of your financial priorities. If you are on a payment plan with your college, be sure to fulfill that obligation in a timely fashion. *You* are the person responsible for seeing that your school bill is paid. The financial aid office is not being held accountable, *you* are. Even if your Aunt Martha said that she would make your tuition payment each month, *you* are still responsible.

Perhaps you have heard that some other student was allowed to make a late payment without penalty. It does not matter; you will be held accountable for making that payment on time. Do not think that a perceived precedent set with another student gives you the right to expect the same treatment. You do not know the whole story of why that exception might have been made. It does not matter how the college handled someone else's situation. You are responsible for paying your school bill, and you are responsible for making those payments on time. Responsible follow-through on your part demonstrates that you are a person of integrity.

If you have received money for educational purposes, be sure to use that money for educational purposes. Let integrity be your guide. The use of some student aid funds for things other than college related expenses can result in you having to return the money.

As much as possible, avoid going into debt while in college. Sometimes acquiring student loans is necessary, but if you do so, be sure to borrow only the amount that you absolutely need. Remember that you will be required to pay back every penny that you borrow, and you will pay it back with interest. Check with your college's financial aid office to learn of options that do not require securing a loan.

What adjustments will you need to make in order to live by a balanced budget while in college?

Health

Success in college requires being healthy in body, soul and spirit. There is virtue in taking care of your body, and the way that you treat your physical being impacts your soul and spirit as well. Your soul includes the mind, will and emotions; the importance of staying sharp in those areas cannot be overstated. Your spirit is that part of you that communes with God and lives forever, even when the body and soul have faded away. If the body and soul are not doing well, your spirit will have difficulty conducting itself to its fullest potential. A holistic approach to health should take all three—body, soul and spirit—into consideration.

The focus here is on maintaining the health of your body. Your body needs proper nutrition. How do you plan to maintain proper nutrition while in college? Your body needs exercise. What is your exercise plan? Your body needs rest. How much rest do you need? How are you going to ensure that you get enough sleep and rest? As far as sleep is concerned, one study at Stanford University concluded that college students typically need at least eight hours of sleep to operate at their optimum level.[27]

In the workspace provided on the following page, start developing your own personalized plan for a healthy lifestyle.

---

[27] William Dement, "Sleepless at Stanford: What All Undergraduates Should Know About How Their Sleeping Lives Affect Their Waking Lives," Stanford University Center of Excellence for the Diagnosis and Treatment of Sleep Disorders, Stanford University, September 1997, accessed May 18, 2015, http://web.stanford.edu/~dement/sleepless.html.

What adjustments will you need to make in the following areas to live a healthy lifestyle while in college?

Nutrition:

Exercise:

Sleep and Rest:

Personal Spirituality

Your priority relationship is your relationship with God. This relationship begins with a spiritual rebirth. The Bible calls it being "born again."[28] Do you have a relationship with God? Have you been born again? If you are not sure, consider the following key passages from the Book of Romans:

Romans 3:10
"As it is written: "There is no one righteous, not even one;"

Romans 3:23
"All have sinned and fall short of the glory of God."

If you desire to receive God's forgiveness and make Jesus Christ the center of your life, your first step is to admit that you are a sinner.

Romans 6:23a
"...The wages of sin is death..."

Sin brings both physical death and spiritual death. Spiritual death alienates us from God, and it will last for all eternity. The Bible teaches that there is a place called the Lake of Fire where lost people will be in torment forever. It is the place where people who are spiritually dead will remain.[29]

Romans 6:23b
"...But the gift of God is eternal life through Jesus Christ our Lord."

Salvation is a gift from God to you! You cannot earn this gift, but you must choose to receive it. Ask God to forgive you of your sins and to give you His gift of eternal life through Jesus.

Romans 5:8
"God demonstrates His own love for us, in that while we were yet sinners Christ died for us!"

When Jesus died on the cross He paid the price for all sin. He took all the sins of the world on Himself on the cross. He bought us out of slavery to sin and death! The only condition is that we believe in Him and what He has done for us.

---

[28] John 3:1-8.

[29] Revelation 20:14-15.

Romans 10:13

"Whoever will call on the name of the Lord will be saved!"

Call out to God in the name of Jesus! He will hear you. He will forgive you. He will save you from your sins. He will give you a new life—an eternal life that begins even in this life.

Romans 10:9, 10

"...If you confess with your mouth Jesus as Lord, and believe in your heart that God raised Jesus from the dead, you shall be saved; for with the heart man believes, resulting in righteousness, and with the mouth he confesses, resulting in salvation."

If you know that God is knocking on your heart's door, ask Him to come into your heart. Jesus said in Revelation 3:20, "Behold I stand at the door and knock, if anyone hears my voice and opens the door, I will come in to him..."

If you do not know how to invite Jesus into your life, praying in sincerity with words like these may help:

Dear God in heaven,

I have been a sinner, but I want to leave my sinful life behind me.

Jesus, I believe you are the Son of God. I believe you came into this world to die on a cross and shed your blood to wash away my sins. I believe that God raised you from the dead, and you have the power to give eternal life.

Wash away my sins. Forgive me. Set me free from the power of sin. Change me from the inside out, so that everything about my life shows how wonderful you really are.

In this moment, I give you my life. I want to live for you for the rest of my life.

Lord Jesus, I receive you as my Lord and Savior. You are my Lord.

If you just now prayed this prayer for the first time in your life, God has heard your prayer and is changing your heart. You are a new creation! Old things have passed away, and your life is being made new.[30] As a follower of Jesus, make it your aim to know Him intimately. Center your life upon His presence.

Spiritual Disciplines

The practice of spiritual disciplines is an important part of personal spirituality. Begin making the following practices part of your daily life:

Prayer. Prayer is communicating with God. Talk to Him often. He is always listening. Whenever you pray, also take time to be still and listen for what He might want to say. Take advantage of student prayer gatherings, but also be sure to maintain your own times of prayer in solitude.

Bible Reading. God speaks through the pages of the Bible. That is why it is called the Word of God. In both the Old and New Testaments it is written, "Man does not live by bread alone, but by every word that comes from the mouth of God."[31]

Cultivate an appetite for God's Word and feed that appetite through daily Bible reading. Numerous Bible reading plans can be found on the Internet. Conduct your own Internet search, and select a plan that best suits you.

Worship. Our highest calling is to be a worshiper of God. We were created to worship God. Gathering with God's people to worship on a regular basis prepares us for worshiping God at all times no matter where we are. Worship is expressing back to God how we esteem His "worth"; that is why some have called it "worth-ship." In other words, in worship we declare that He is worthy of all our love, affection and devotion.

There are many ways to worship God. We worship Him with singing. We worship Him with musical instruments. We worship Him with shouts of praise. We worship Him with prayers of adoration and thanksgiving. We worship Him with dancing. We worship Him with

---

[30] 2 Corinthians 5:17.

[31] Deuteronomy 8:3; Matthew 4:4.

the lifting of our hands. We worship Him with the clapping of our hands. We worship Him through giving. We worship Him through serving. We worship Him by simply turning the affections of our hearts toward Him. Worship Him more joyfully than you ever have before. Worship Him with more intensity as well as with more sincerity. Worship Him with all that you are and all that you have.

In a Christian college you should be given many opportunities to worship God corporately. Make it your aim to attend every chapel service. Make it your aim to attend every church service. Make it your aim to participate in every prayer meeting. If your college is taking a group to a worship concert, go with them. Take advantage of every opportunity to worship God.

Meditation. Meditation is the practice of becoming quiet before God, focusing your thoughts upon Him, resting in His presence and listening for His voice. This powerful spiritual discipline is also known as "soaking" or "waiting upon the Lord." Set yourself apart from distractions for thirty minutes or an hour. Take nothing with you except your Bible, a journal and some instrumental music. Turn on the music, relax, and wait upon the Lord. Fix your thoughts upon Him. Listen for His voice. This is not a time for you to produce *for* God; this is your time to receive *from* Him.

Fellowship. God did not design the Christian life to even function properly apart from relationship with other Christians. You need fellowship—the sharing of life with other believers. You need the other members of the Body of Christ, and they need you. In areas where you may be weak, someone else in your life can be strong. Similarly, in areas where you are strong, you might be God's answer to someone else's prayer for help. We need one another.

It is not just important for you to know others in your college; you have got to also *make yourself known*. I am not talking about showing off or selfishly trying to draw attention. I am talking about showing up for social opportunities whenever they avail themselves. Be where people are. Take a risk. Take the first step to introduce yourself to others, and ask them to share their story.

Make new friends, and begin the wonderful journey of doing life together. Pray for one another. Bear one another's burdens. Serve one another. May you and all of your new college friends learn what it means to be Christian together.

Your Response

As strange as it may seem, some have found that Christian college can be a place to easily backslide. Attending Bible and ministry classes day after day cannot replace the need for you to cultivate your own personal walk with God. You may be constantly surrounded by Christian things, but still *you* need to pray, *you* need to worship, *you* need to read your Bible and *you* need to live in intentional community with other believers.

Take a few moments to review this final section on Personal Spirituality. What do you think God is saying to you regarding this area of your life? Jot down what you think He is saying. Then write a short prayer expressing to Him your response. Let Him know your desire to grow spiritually while attending this college.

What do you think God is saying to you regarding your own spiritual growth?

> **Write a short prayer, expressing to God your response to what He is saying. Express your desire to grow spiritually while attending this college.**

CHAPTER 7
BEST ACADEMIC PRACTICES

You have chosen to devote several years of your life to prepare for a vocational or ministerial pursuit. If this time in college is to be an investment into your future, then it makes sense to engage in the practices that are best for helping you to achieve your goals. In this chapter we will explore what many have found to be the best academic practices for achieving success in the college experience.

Reading

Reading and studying will define the greater part of your life while in college. The amount of required reading can seem overwhelming, but it does not have to be that way—not if you begin this work early in the semester and follow through with a disciplined reading and studying plan. Be in the habit of carrying a book with you wherever you go, and convert your times of idleness into opportunities to absorb the book's contents.

How to Read a Book

Consider reading each book in three stages: preview, view and review.

1. Preview. When reading a textbook for a college course, prior to the first class session, preview the book. Read whatever is written on the front cover, back cover and inside flaps. Scan down through the Table of Contents. Read the Foreword, Preface and Introduction.

If time permits, preview the book more thoroughly. For each chapter beyond the Introduction, read the first paragraph. Then read the first and last sentence of each subsequent paragraph and the final paragraph of each chapter. Be sure to also read any part of the text the publisher has highlighted or set apart in a text box. Finally, read the concluding chapter in its entirety.

2. View. As soon as you receive your course syllabus, take note of readings that have been assigned for the textbook. Follow the syllabus schedule, and complete each reading assignment accordingly. Read each assigned section in its entirety. Mark the points in the text that appear to be especially important. Jot down any questions that come to mind as you are reading. If you will do this work prior to each class, you should be well prepared to participate in classroom discussions.

3. Review. If classroom lectures are coordinated with the reading assignments, be sure to review the text after the corresponding lecture has been delivered. Ask yourself, "How does this material relate to what I have already learned or experienced? How will this material help me to succeed in my personal and vocational development?" Review and reflection will solidify concepts in your mind. As you prepare for quizzes and examinations, reviewing marks and notes that you have made on the pages should also enhance your learning.

Listening and Note-taking

Listening to lectures and taking notes are skills that can be developed over time. If you are easily distracted, you can retrain your brain to habitually focus.

Listening with Honor

Listen with an attitude of honor for the speaker or instructor. When you listen with an attitude of honor, you increase the likelihood that you are going to benefit from the lecture. Also be aware that the instructor can easily discern the attitude of students. When students listen with an attitude of disrespect, it hinders the teacher.

Go into each class session with this attitude: "This place is where I *want* to be today. I *need* this lecture, and I am going to benefit from it. This instructor has something important to say, and I am going to listen carefully."

Knowing that your attitude affects learning, please be aware of your body language and what it is communicating during each class session. Travis Bradberry, a leadership contributor to Forbes.com, notes a number of common body language mistakes to avoid—eight relating to conduct in the classroom:

1. Avoiding eye contact,
2. Slouching,
3. Folding arms,
4. Looking down,
5. Angling body away from others,
6. Fidgeting and touching hair,
7. Glancing at the clock and
8. Frowning or scowling.[32]

Taking Notes

Every student must take responsibility for the content of classroom lectures, reading assignments and presentations. Any time a lecture is delivered, expect to do some note-taking. Any time a presentation is made, something will need to be written down. If a reading assignment is given, take notes as you read. If handouts are distributed, read them, highlight key points and be sure to keep those documents in a place where you can easily retrieve them.

Each class that you take should have its own notebook. Some prefer spiral notebooks, some prefer three-ring binders and others prefer typing their notes on a portable electronic device. Making audio recordings of class sessions and transcribing lectures afterwards can be

---

[32] Travis Bradberry "10 Worst Body Language Mistakes," *Forbes*, accessed July 3, 2015, http://www3.forbes.com/leadership/10-worst-body-language-mistakes/2/.

helpful, but if you choose this method, make sure that you have your instructor's permission to do so.

Knowing what parts of a classroom presentation to write down is a skill that you will develop over time. Obviously you cannot write down every word that comes from the professor's mouth, so how do you decide what to record?

When a teacher delivers a lecture from a prepared outline, it is easier to take notes. Write down the main points of outlined sequences that you may hear, introduced by words such as "first," "second" and "third." After each main point, listen for supporting points, and write them down in a way that visually reminds you that those subordinate points support the major idea recorded above them.

If the instructor projects something on a screen, write it down. If he or she writes it on the board, write it down. Listen for key places, names, titles, events and dates; write them down. Pay special attention when the teacher makes statements like these:

"This is important."

"Remember this."

"You need to know this."

"Be sure to write this down."

"This will be on the test."

After class, review the notes you have written. Compare notes with others who were in the session, and fill in any gaps that may exist in your note-taking. Rewriting your notes can also help to bring clarity and to solidify concepts in your mind.

Research

Research is an essential part of the college experience. Approach research with an attitude that says, "I am on my way to becoming an expert on this subject."

The college library will be the primary place where you will conduct research. Early in your college experience spend some time in the library, and learn how to access the library's catalog of resources. Look up a few of the supplemental texts listed in the syllabi of your courses, and retrieve them from the shelves where they are located. Browse through the periodicals, journals and reference materials.

Most college libraries provide an orientation to the library's use. If your library does not provide an orientation or if you somehow missed it, ask someone on the library staff to show you around and to explain how to utilize the services that are available.

Writing

Christians bring something distinctive into the writing experience. One might easily understand that *what* a Christian writes will often differ from what a non-Christian would write. However, the difference is not only in the content. The difference is also found in *how* Christians write and the reason *why* they write.

Why Christians Write

Why do we write? We all have a story to tell. Our stories are important—not only to us but also to those who will hear or read them. Your personal story is a testimony to how God has encountered you. Your story has a bearing on how you view everything. Experience affects our lens. God is involved in our lives.

Writing is an opportunity to experience the grace of God flowing to you and through you in a way that is customized to who you are. You should write, because no one else can write the way you write. There is uniqueness to what God has made you to be. You are unique for a purpose. There is a life message in you. You are a living epistle. Who you are colors what you write.

God wants to communicate to you and through you. The Holy Spirit speaks through the writings of God's people. When the Holy Spirit is upon you as you write, you will be amazed at what ends up on the page. In days to come you will look back in amazement at things you have written, and you will say, "Did *I* write that?"

As you write, understanding emerges. Things you had not previously thought about come to surface. You grow in knowledge as you write. When you write, you are co-creating with God. Human creativity came from God. Do not underestimate the significance of this creativity. While you are in college, you will write things that will one day be the beginnings of speeches, sermons, screenplays, books and articles—items that will be published.

How Christians Write

How do we write as Christians? We have the opportunity to write in the Spirit. We often say, "I cannot do it without God," but God has chosen not to do it without us!

If we are going to do anything in the Spirit, then we need to cultivate a lifestyle of hosting the presence of God. Make yourself aware of God's presence before you start writing. Steward His presence. Listen for His voice. Do what you see the Father doing. Soak in His presence. Spend some time writing in your journal. Write in His presence as an act of worship, and what you produce will be transformative.

Do not be afraid of your imagination. God will use both Spirit-led and non Spirit-led imaginations. Keep the canvas of your imagination clean so that God can paint His pictures there.

Overcoming Writer's Block

Learn to overcome writer's block. Take a short walk, and get some fresh air. Remove the clutter and noise from your work and study environment. Put away distracting and nonessential electronic devices. An Internet search will reveal numerous additional ways to address this problem.

Perfectionism can sometimes interfere in the writing process. Begin to function by *the rule of three*. Instead of trying to think of the *one* perfect thing to say, try to think of *three* things to say. This practice will break you out of perfectionism. After you have jotted down three things, then you can pick the best one.

Avoiding Plagiarism

Plagiarism is the act of using or closely imitating another person's thoughts or work without crediting the original author. It is the intentional or unintentional representation of that author's thoughts or work as though it were one's own.[33]

It is important to make yourself fully aware of your college's plagiarism policy. Any college will require that all your academic work be the result of your own thought and research. When using ideas and statements that did not originate with you, appropriately citing your sources is absolutely necessary. If you feel unsure as to what may or may not constitute plagiarism on a particular assignment, consult with your instructor on the matter before submitting it.

How serious is plagiarism? Plagiarism is cheating. Plagiarism is theft. Plagiarism is dishonest. Plagiarism is lying. Plagiarism is illegal. Plagiarism is sin.

Using another person's thoughts or material without crediting that person is costly. In school, it will cost you a failing grade. It could even result in failing the whole course or even being suspended from college. If you fail that course, how much did you pay for that course? Whatever that amount is, that is how much plagiarizing on that one assignment will cost you. If you are suspended from college, how much has that one instance of cheating on that paper cost you? You are looking at a potential loss of thousands of dollars.

In society, plagiarism is costly. Even minor offenses may be fined $150,000 or more. Beyond the monetary aspect of this matter, the shame and disgrace of this offense may never be forgotten by the public, even if the original author forgives you.

"But what if I don't get caught?" someone may ask. First, do not gamble on the possibility of not being caught. Most college professors are experienced and very good at detecting plagiarism, and they have

---

[33] "Plagiarism," Dictionary.com, accessed September 12, 2015, http://dictionary.reference.com/browse/plagiarism.

access to technologies designed to identify instances of intellectual property theft. Second, even if you do not get caught, why would you want to live your life outside of the favor of God? Why would you want to numb your own conscience against the severity of this transgression? The internal deterioration of your own character is not worth it.

There are a number of common misconceptions regarding plagiarism that warrant the following points of clarification:

1. If you unintentionally plagiarize, it is still plagiarism.

2. If you restate another person's thoughts entirely in your own words but do not cite the source of those ideas, it is still plagiarism.

3. If you use material that is in the public domain and do not cite the source, it is still plagiarism.

4. If you use material that *you* authored for another writing assignment but do not cite your previous work as a source, it is still plagiarism.

In short, do not plagiarize. Copying someone else's work may seem like a short-cut, but by doing so, you are depriving yourself of the opportunity to develop as a researcher and writer. Besides, the world needs to read and hear *your* thoughts, not the stolen thoughts of others.

If you are guilty of having plagiarized in the past, repentance is in order. Admit that you have sinned, ask God for forgiveness, and make a quality decision to not plagiarize again.

Avoiding Common Errors

Anyone can become blind to their own writing errors. Let someone else review your written work before submitting it. Train yourself to avoid the following common writing errors. If your instructor provides examples, use the space beneath each item to jot down a few notes. If your instructor does not present examples, go to the websites indicated in the footnote.[34]

---

[34] Andrea A. Lunsford, "20 Most Common Errors," *The Everyday Writer*, accessed August 13, 2015, http:// bcs.bedfordstmartins.com/ everyday_writer/

Common Writing Errors

1. No comma after an introductory word, phrase or clause

2. Missing comma in a compound sentence

3. Wrong word choice

   "Its" or "It's"

   "Who" or "Whom"

20errors/; Christina Sterbenz, "The 11 Most Common Grammatical Mistakes And How To Avoid Them," *Business Insider*, September 12, 2013, accessed August 14, 2015, http://www.businessinsider.com/11-common-grammatical-mistakes-and-how-to-avoid-them-2013-9.

"Me," "Myself" or "I"

"Lie" or "Lay"

Other

4. Wrong or missing verb ending

5. Comma splice

6. Sentence fragment

7. Lack of subject-verb agreement

8. Spelling errors

9. Capitalization errors

10. Ending Sentences with Prepositions

Quizzes and Tests

In your college experience, you will encounter many quizzes and tests[35] along the way. Quizzes and tests measure *what* you have learned. They are not designed to indicate your level of intelligence, you personal worth or your ability to succeed. To perform at your optimum level on a quiz or test, apply yourself to learning.

Review the syllabus for each course to become familiar with expectations for testing. Quizzes typically measure comprehension of small amounts of information learned over a short period of time. Successful completion of quizzes often prepares students for the successful completion of more substantial tests or examinations.

Some teachers may administer a quiz every week. Others may space them further apart. Without warning an instructor may administer unannounced "pop quizzes," saying something like, "Put away all books and notes. Take out a piece of paper and a pen. It is time to take a quiz!"

Tests or examinations usually cover more content than quizzes. Most teachers will give plenty of advance warning when a test has been scheduled. Check your syllabus, note the dates, and enter them into your personal calendar.

Types of Testing

Quizzes and tests are comprised of questions falling under two classifications: objective questions and subjective questions.

Objective Questions. Multiple-choice, true-false, matching and most fill-in-the-blank items are examples of objective questions. Objective questions have only one correct answer or one set of correct answers. They are fact-based and are not subject to the student's opinion or personal perspective.

---

[35] In this context, "tests" and "examinations" are synonymous terms.

Subjective Questions. Essay questions and some fill-in-the-blank items are examples of subjective questions. While they may require the recall of specific facts and concepts taught in class, they also allow the students' responses to be colored by their personal perspectives, writing styles and creative abilities. Knowledge gained throughout the course and even beyond the scope of the course can often inform a response to a subjective question.

Preparing for Tests

The best way to prepare for a quiz or a test is to become thoroughly familiar with the material. The manner in which you study, pay attention in class and take notes paves the way for test preparation. If you are consistent in these areas on a weekly basis, your preparation will be much easier.

Reviewing and Summarizing. Preparation for tests involves reviewing and summarizing reading material and notes taken in class. After you have worked through assigned readings, type a summary of the material you have read. After you have saved your summary, prepare a second version that includes the integration of content from notes you have taken in class. Include your own thoughts and reflections as well.

Disciplined note-taking during class lectures will place you at a great advantage when test time comes upon you. Review the notes you have written. As suggested earlier in the section on Listening and Note-taking, compare notes with others who are in your class, and fill in any gaps that may exist in your own notes. Rewriting your notes can also help to bring clarity as you review.

Memorizing. Preparation for tests sometimes involves the memorization of key formulas, rules, names, dates, places, events, terms, definitions, quotes, sequences and lists. Of course, Bible, theology and ministry courses may involve the memorization of Scripture. Memorization can be aided through repeated review, word association, visualization and the use of mnemonic devices.

With your study notes in hand, identify the parts that need to be memorized. Then begin to review those parts, repeating them aloud. You may find it helpful to conduct this exercise with a friend. Have your friend check your accuracy as you recite the content you are attempting to memorize. Repetition is an indispensable part of memorization.

One student in my Success in College class reported that he likes to store lists of words in his memory by forming acronyms using the first letter of each word in the list. A good example of this technique is the FORD acronym that I noted in the chapter entitled, "Relationships." Each letter in the word, FORD, triggers the mind to recall these four conversation-starting topics: family, occupation, recreation and dreams. This same student said that he also makes up songs using the words, facts or concepts that he needs to remember. Songs are easier to remember than mere words.

Word association and visualization can also be helpful in memorization. A term or concept may remind you of a person, place or thing. As you review that concept, visualize it as set within a mental picture of that person, place or thing. Then plug into that internal image additional elements associated with the content you are trying to commit to memory.

Some people find the "mnemonic peg system"[36] helpful for committing lists of things to memory. This system provides a way to always have a ready-made method for memorizing a list of ten items. First, permanently install the system in your brain by memorizing the following list:

- One, run
- Two, zoo
- Three, tree
- Four, door

---

[36] Henry Herdson is credited with developing the mnemonic peg system. Kenneth L. Higbee, *Your Memory: How it Works and How to Improve It*, 2nd ed. (New York: Da Capo Press, 2001), 158.

- Five, hive
- Six, sick
- Seven, heaven
- Eight, gate
- Nine, wine
- Ten, den

The second part of installing this mnemonic system in your mind is to create a mental picture of each word or "peg" associated with the numbers in the list:

- **One, run.** Visualize one horse running. Mentally place the item you are trying to remember on the back of the horse.
- **Two, zoo.** Visualize two monkeys in a cage in the zoo. Picture the two monkeys fighting over the item you are trying to commit to memory.
- **Three, tree.** Visualize a tree. The item you want to remember is hanging from a branch on the tree.
- **Four, door.** Visualize a revolving door. The item you want to remember is getting stuck in the door.
- **Five, hive.** Visualize a bee hive. Picture a miniature version of the item you are trying to remember; it is flying like a bee in and out of the hive.
- **Six, sick.** Visualize a patient sick in bed. A nurse is standing by the bed administering an injection to the patient using a huge syringe. The item you want to remember is in the syringe, and the nurse is injecting that item into the patient.
- **Seven, heaven.** Visualize a staircase ascending straight up into heaven. As you look up the staircase, the item you want to remember is tumbling down the staircase.
- **Eight, gate.** Visualize a gate. The item you are committing to memory is coming through the gate.
- **Nine, wine.** Visualize a bottle of wine. The item you want to remember is in the bottle.
- **Ten, den.** Visualize Daniel in the den of lions (Daniel 6). In the biblical story, God shut the mouths of the lions so that they could not harm Daniel. Imagine that the reason the lions could not move their mouths was because the item you are trying to remember is stuck in each of their mouths.

Each time you use this system, the "pegs" ("run," "zoo," "tree," etc.) never change. Only the items you commit to memory change with each new list that you are attempting to memorize. Try using this system the next time you prepare your grocery list.

There are limitations to using such memorization aids. Mnemonic devices are good for holding lists in short-term memory, but they are not beneficial for gaining understanding of new concepts. Once again, becoming thoroughly familiar with the material is the best way to prepare.

Taking the Test

After a good night of sleep, wake up the next morning, put a smile on your face, and get ready for the day with an attitude that says, "I am going to prevail when I take that test!" Of course, it is assumed that you have prepared.

When you are taking a test, what do you do, if you do not know the answer? Usually it is not a good idea just to leave the answer blank. Trying one or more of the following actions may prove helpful:

1. Replay in your mind how the question's topic was covered in class or in your reading assignments. Think through points related to the subject. This mental review may cause the answer to become obvious.

2. Skip the question, and come back later. Other questions in the examination may help to trigger in your mind the correct answer.

3. If it is a multiple choice question, eliminate the choices that are clearly incorrect, and then make an intelligent guess.

4. If it is an essay question, anything you write down that is within the general area of what is being asked is better than not writing anything at all. If you leave it blank, you will definitely get it wrong. Once you start writing, the remembrance of what you heard in class or read in your textbook may come to mind.

5. Ask for clarification.

After the Test

If you perform poorly on a test, do not beat up on yourself. Neither should you just throw the test away and forget about it. Authors Carol J. Carter and Joyce Bishop suggest that students do the following after they have completed their examinations:

1. Consider what you could have done better.
2. Fill in your knowledge gaps.
3. Ask your professor what you could have done better.
4. Reconsider your approach to studying.[37]

Additional Insights

Having worked through this chapter, note one stated practice that seemed the most relevant or helpful to you. Then note some of your own ideas. What additional insights do you have regarding best academic practices—keys to college success that may not have been mentioned here? Be prepared to share these thoughts with your class or study group.

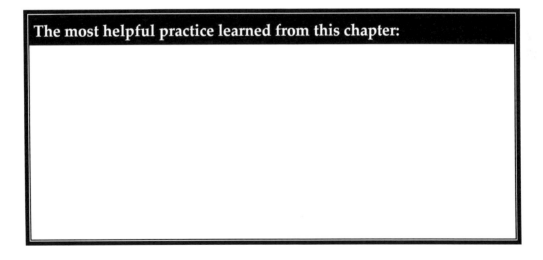

The most helpful practice learned from this chapter:

---

[37] Carol J. Carter, Joyce Bishop and Sarah Lyman Kravits, *Keys to Success Quick* (Columbus, Ohio: Pearson, 2011).

Additional helpful practices not mentioned in this chapter:

Chapter 8
Your Learning Style

Students become more successful in their studies when they are aware of the ways in which they learn best. Everyone functions with a combination of learning styles, but most people have one dominant approach to learning. A person may use a particular learning technique in one setting and a different one in another circumstance. However, a preferred mode typically comes to surface over time.

What are learning styles? Marlene LeFever, author of *Learning Styles*, defines a learning style as the way in which a person perceives things best. It also involves how that person processes or uses what has been received.[38]

What are students to do if a college course requires a learning technique with which they are not comfortable? The good news is that people are not eternally locked in to their dominant pattern of learning. Learning styles can be developed. Weaker abilities can be strengthened, and stronger ones can be further developed as well.[39]

The Learning and Skills Research Centre in London reports there are at least seventy-one learning style theories.[40] In this text we will consider two—one from Indiana University and the other from

---

[38] Marlene Lefever, *Learning Styles* (David C. Cook, 1995).

[39] "Overview of Learning Styles," Learning Styles Online, accessed September 12, 2015, http://www.learning-styles-online.com/overview/.

[40] F. Coffield, D. Moseley, E. Hall and K. Ecclestone, *Learning Styles and Pedagogy in Post-16 Learning. A Systematic and Critical Review* (London: Learning and Skills Research Centre, 2004).

Marlene Lefever, Vice President for Educational Development at David C. Cook—a Christian publishing company.

Theory 1: Three Learning Styles

In an article entitled, "Three Learning Styles,"[41] Bepko Learning Center[42] of Indiana University presents three learning styles and their common characteristics. The following is *a modified adaptation* of the model combined with corresponding suggestions for learning:

1. Visual

Common Characteristics:

- Learns best by observing or by being shown
- Learns best when teaching includes the use of visual objects and graphics
- Learns best in lectures by reading the body language of the speaker
- Remembers written information

Suggestions for Learning:

- Convert your class notes into drawings, charts or other graphic representations.
- Avoid visual distractions while in the classroom or while studying.

---

[41] "Three Learning Styles," Academic Enrichment, BEPKO Learning Center, Indiana University-Purdue University Indianapolis, accessed September 12, 2015, http://blc.uc.iupui.edu/Academic-Enrichment/Study-Skills/Learning-Styles/3-Learning-Styles.

[42] According the Bepko Learning Center website, "The Bepko Learning Center of IUPUI (formerly called the Student Mentor and Resource Center) is the culmination of the vision and courage of Dr. Herman Blake, Dr. Scott Evenbeck, Dr. William Plater, and Tonja Eagan." "A Brief History of the Unit," BEPKO Learning Center, accessed November 14, 2015, http://blc.uc.iupui.edu/About-Us/Program-History.

- Consider the big picture or context first; then study the details.
- Use flash cards to study vocabulary and concise pieces of information.

2. Auditory

Common Characteristics:

- Learns best by listening and speaking
- Learns best by being told how to do things
- Often learns better with instrumental music playing in the background

Suggestions for Learning:

- Record lectures, and listen to them later.
- Read written material aloud, or repeat it aloud in your own words.
- Discuss course content with another student or in a study group.
- Listen to instrumental music while studying.

3. Kinesthetic

Common Characteristics:

- Learns best through hands-on instructional methods—learning by doing
- Learns better while engaged in physical activity
- Generally proficient in math and science
- Would rather *demonstrate* how to do something than verbally explain it
- Usually prefers group work

Suggestions for Learning:

- Take frequent study breaks.
- Engage in physical activity while learning new concepts or information. For instance, chew gum, stand or pace while studying or reading.
- If the lesson involves learning physical actions or procedures, activate your newly acquired knowledge by putting it into practice.
- Take classes that involve physical projects, demonstrations and fieldwork.[43]

Which of the three learning styles noted in this section best describes your learning preference?

☐ Visual

☐ Auditory

☐ Kinesthetic

Give an example of a time when you learned best in that way.

---

[43] "Three Learning Styles," Academic Enrichment, Bepko Learning Center, Indiana University - Purdue University, Indianapolis.

Theory 2: Four Learning Styles

In her book, *Learning Styles: Reaching Everyone God Gave You*,[44] Marlene Lefever presents four basic learning styles: the imaginative learner, the analytic learner, the common sense learner and the dynamic learner.

Dynamic Learner	Imaginative Learner
Common Sense Learner	Analytic Learner

The Imaginative Learner

Imaginative Learners make use of their life experience as a foundation for gaining new knowledge. They ask, "Why do I need to know this?"

Students who are imaginative learners learn best through observation and reflection. They find that they increase in knowledge and skill through activities such as group interaction, role-play, group singing and storytelling. Imaginative learners also enjoy arts and crafts, and they are often good at artistic interpretation.

The Analytic Learner

Analytic Learners are very rational and sequential thinkers. They want to know what the experts think and say. They ask, "What do I need to know?"

Students who are analytic learners find that they learn best through programmed instruction. They perform at their optimum level when their educational experience includes activities such as lectures, self study, reading, research projects and focused class discussions.

---

[44] Marlene Lefever.

The Common Sense Learner

Common Sense learners experiment to see if what they have learned really works. They ask, "How does this work?"

Students who are common sense learners learn best in the practical application aspect of education. They thrive in an environment where learning involves problem-solving and hands-on assignments. For common sense learners, even games of skill can enhance the educational experience.

The Dynamic Learner

Dynamic Learners learn simply for the fun of learning. They enjoy coming up with creative and unique applications for what they have learned. They ask, "What can this become?"

Students who are dynamic learners find that they learn best when learning requires innovative thinking. They enjoy activities such as wrestling with moral dilemmas, working through case studies, brainstorming and participating in open-ended discussions.

God made each person unique; there is no other person quite like you. Part of your uniqueness includes your particular learning style. As you learn more about how God made you, you gain an appreciation for the way that you learn and are enabled to maximize on the potential of your personal learning style. When you understand the diversity of learning styles among people, that understanding will one day help you in areas of life outside the educational context. Consider how understanding each person's learning style can help you to work with groups, supervise teams and even improve family relationships.

Your Learning Style

Which of the four learning styles noted in this section best describes your learning preference? Why?

☐ Imaginative Learner
☐ Analytic Learner
☐ Common Sense Learner
☐ Dynamic Learner

Why? Explain why you made your selection. Provide an example of a time when you learned best in that way.

Strengthening Your Learning Abilities

While helping you to identify your preferred learning style, this chapter has also uncovered approaches to learning that do not work well with you. You can become stronger in those areas of weakness. In light of what you have gained in this lesson, how can you become more adept in those areas?

What can you do to strengthen your learning abilities?

Chapter 9
Relationships

God the Father is relational. He exists in relationship with His Son and with the Holy Spirit. He exists in relationship with His heavenly creation—angels and other living beings. He exists in relationship with His earthly creation—every living creature. He exists in relationship with all men and women throughout the earth. They are His creation, and He is their Creator, whether they choose to acknowledge Him as such or not. He is in relationship with all who have been redeemed by the blood of Christ Jesus; He is their Father, and they are His sons and daughters.

God is indeed relational, and since He created you *in His image*, you are also a relational being. You were not made to be alone. In fact, after God created Adam, He said concerning the man He had created that it was not good for man to be alone.[45]

Knowing that a solitary existence would not be good for Adam, God made a companion for him. Her name was Eve—the mother of all the living.[46] When God brought Eve to Adam to be his companion,[47] with that act He established the institution of marriage.[48] Then with the births of Cain, Abel and their siblings, God instituted the human family. From that point forward the relational order for mankind included sons and daughters, brothers and sisters, fathers and mothers.

---

[45] Genesis 2:18.

[46] Genesis 3:20.

[47] Genesis 2:22.

[48] Genesis 2:24.

As time progressed, the human family grew, and the many branches of Adam's race became known by their tribal identities. Each tribe and nation was defined by their genealogy—their ancestral connection back to a "father" and ultimately back to the beginning. The concept of covenant friendships emerged as people separated by tribal and national boundaries sought to form agreements and cooperative pursuits together. Although they were not closely connected in a biological sense, they became friends—even like brothers and sisters to one another.

Sin brought disruption to the harmony of relationships in the earth, but Jesus came to deal with the sin problem. Through the blood of Jesus, the broken relationship between God and man was healed, and that healing has become accessible to any who would respond to His grace. Through the blood of Jesus, the sin that had broken relationships between the people of earth was also defeated, and that victory has been made available to any who would respond to grace. Offenders can now repent and be forgiven, and those who have been offended now have the power to partner with God in forgiving and releasing their offenders from their guilt and shame.[49]

The Bible is full of wisdom for cultivating, forming, stewarding, protecting, strengthening and advancing healthy relationships. That wisdom applies to all relationships. Wisdom is available in the pages of God's Word for man's relationship with God. There is wisdom for family relationships, church relationships, professional relationships and international relationships. There is wisdom for relationships between races, relationships between genders, relationships between sinners and saints, and relationships between friends. Take a year to read through your Bible, and as you do so, take note of the many ways that God aims to help us make relationships healthier.

---

[49] James 5:16.

A Spiritual Family[50]

Students arrive at college from diverse family backgrounds. Many do not come from healthy family environments while others do. It is important to honor and respect your family back home; however, in the Christian college environment you may have opportunity to identify new spiritual fathers and mothers—teachers, leaders and mentors whom God has appointed to model His love and to speak wisdom into your life.

Whenever God brings a person into a new life-season, that transition brings with it new relationships. As you experience spiritual transformation, you may find that you can no longer retain some of your previous relationships—especially if those relational connections have had a tendency to draw you away from heaven's purposes. Ask God for friends who are passionate for Jesus. Then be proactive, and be a friend to others. Many of the friends that you make in college will be friends for life.

In the opening of this chapter, we considered the genesis of the human family. The relational dynamics of biological or adoptive families inform how we should function as spiritual families. Similarly, the dynamics of spiritual families inform how we should relate as biological or adoptive families. When we look at how the family of God is to function, we can learn some things about how our biological families or even our adoptive families should function.

Ideally your Christian college experience should afford you the opportunity to experience life as a member of God's family. Even if no one reaches out to you as a spiritual father or mother, or as a spiritual brother or sister, God has empowered *you* to take the initiative to reach out to someone in brotherly love. You have the power to position

---

[50] In this section, "A Spiritual Family," portions have been adapted from the core values of Bethel School of Supernatural Ministry in Redding, California.

yourself as a son or daughter toward some godly spiritual father or mother. We can intentionally create family wherever we go.

> **In the next several sections, an extensive amount of scriptures will be presented. Highlight or underscore the parts that seem especially relevant to you. Write your own notes and reflections in the margins.**

You Belong

Always know that you really belong. You *do* have a place at the table of this royal family. Ponder the following passages, and consider how they relate to the family aspect of the Christian life:

1 John 3:1
3 See what great love the Father has lavished on us, that we should be called children of God! And that is what we are! The reason the world does not know us is that it did not know him.

Luke 8:20-21
20 Someone told him [Jesus], "Your mother and brothers are standing outside, wanting to see you." 21 He replied, "My mother and brothers are those who hear God's word and put it into practice."

Ephesians 2:19
19 Consequently, you are no longer foreigners and strangers, but fellow citizens with God's people and also members of his household.

Loyalty in Times of Failure

As members of God's family, our aim is to be loyal, and loyalty is proven most authentic when people fail. When people sin, we do not abandon them; rather, we make every effort to restore them. No matter what people do, our standard is loving confrontation, forgiveness and restoration. Consider the following passages:

Matthew 18:15

15 "If your brother or sister sins, go and point out their fault, just between the two of you. If they listen to you, you have won them over.

John 8:2-11

2 At dawn he [Jesus] appeared again in the temple courts, where all the people gathered around him, and he sat down to teach them. 3 The teachers of the law and the Pharisees brought in a woman caught in adultery. They made her stand before the group 4 and said to Jesus, "Teacher, this woman was caught in the act of adultery. 5 In the Law Moses commanded us to stone such women. Now what do you say?" 6 They were using this question as a trap, in order to have a basis for accusing him. But Jesus bent down and started to write on the ground with his finger. 7 When they kept on questioning him, he straightened up and said to them, "Let any one of you who is without sin be the first to throw a stone at her." 8 Again he stooped down and wrote on the ground. 9 At this, those who heard began to go away one at a time, the older ones first, until only Jesus was left, with the woman still standing there. 10 Jesus straightened up and asked her, "Woman, where are they? Has no one condemned you?" 11 "No one, sir," she said. "Then neither do I condemn you," Jesus declared. "Go now and leave your life of sin."

Galatians 6:1

1 Brothers and sisters, if someone is caught in a sin, you who live by the Spirit should restore that person gently. But watch yourselves, or you also may be tempted.

Matthew 18:21-22

21 Then Peter came to Jesus and asked, "Lord, how many times shall I forgive my brother or sister who sins against me? Up to seven times?"

22 Jesus answered, "I tell you, not seven times, but seventy-seven times."

Seeking the Good of Others

As the family of God, we seek the good of others. We are not motivated by selfishness or personal gain. The New Testament conveys a strong and consistent message that followers of Christ are to relate to one another in humility, honor, empathy and love:

Philippians 2:3-16

3 Do nothing out of selfish ambition or vain conceit. Rather, in humility value others above yourselves, 4 not looking to your own interests but each of you to the interests of the others. 5 In your relationships with one another, have the same mindset as Christ Jesus:

6 Who, being in very nature God, did not consider equality with God something to be used to his own advantage; 7 rather, he made himself nothing by taking the very nature of a servant, being made in human likeness. 8 And being found in appearance as a man, he humbled himself by becoming obedient to death—even death on a cross!

9 Therefore God exalted him to the highest place and gave him the name that is above every name, 10 that at the name of Jesus every knee should bow, in heaven and on earth and under the earth, 11 and every tongue acknowledge that Jesus Christ is Lord, to the glory of God the Father.

12 Therefore, my dear friends, as you have always obeyed—not only in my presence, but now much more in my absence—continue to work out your salvation with fear and trembling, 13 for it is God who works in you to will and to act in order to fulfill his good purpose.

14 Do everything without grumbling or arguing, 15 so that you may become blameless and pure, "children of God without fault in a warped and crooked generation." Then you will shine among them like stars in the sky 16 as you hold firmly to the word of life. And then I will be able to boast on the day of Christ that I did not run or labor in vain.

Romans 12:10

10 Be devoted to one another in love. Honor one another above yourselves.

Ephesians 5:21

21 Submit to one another out of reverence for Christ.

Galatians 6:2
2 Carry each other's burdens, and in this way you will fulfill the law of Christ.

Galatians 6:10
10 Therefore, as we have opportunity, let us do good to all people, especially to those who belong to the family of believers.

1 Peter 2:17
17 Show proper respect to everyone; love the family of believers….

Galatians 5:13c
13c Serve one another humbly in love.

Romans 12:13-18
13 Share with the Lord's people who are in need. Practice hospitality. 14 Bless those who persecute you; bless and do not curse. 15 Rejoice with those who rejoice; mourn with those who mourn. 16 Live in harmony with one another. Do not be proud, but be willing to associate with people of low position. Do not be conceited. 17 Do not repay anyone evil for evil. Be careful to do what is right in the eyes of everyone. 18 If it is possible, as far as it depends on you, live at peace with everyone.

1 Peter 3:8
8 Finally, all of you, be like-minded, be sympathetic, love one another, be compassionate and humble.

1 Peter 5:5
5 In the same way, you who are younger, submit yourselves to your elders. All of you, clothe yourselves with humility toward one another, because, "God opposes the proud but shows favor to the humble."

A Powerful Family

God's family is a powerful family. As a member of this family, you have access to this power:

Joel 2:28
28 "And afterward,
I will pour out my Spirit on all people.

Your sons and daughters will prophesy,
your old men will dream dreams,
your young men will see visions."

Acts 2:1-2

2 When the day of Pentecost came, they were all together in one place. 2 Suddenly a sound like the blowing of a violent wind came from heaven and filled the whole house where they were sitting.[51]

Matthew 18:20

20 For where two or three gather in my name, there am I with them."

Ephesians 3:14-21

14 For this reason I kneel before the Father, 15 from whom every family in heaven and on earth derives its name. 16 I pray that out of his glorious riches he may strengthen you with power through his Spirit in your inner being, 17 so that Christ may dwell in your hearts through faith. And I pray that you, being rooted and established in love, 18 may have power, together with all the Lord's holy people, to grasp how wide and long and high and deep is the love of Christ, 19 and to know this love that surpasses knowledge—that you may be filled to the measure of all the fullness of God. 20 Now to him who is able to do immeasurably more than all we ask or imagine, according to his power that is at work within us, 21 to him be glory in the church and in Christ Jesus throughout all generations, for ever and ever! Amen.

Matthew 6:9

9 "This, then, is how you should pray:
'Our Father in heaven,
hallowed be your name.'"

What It Looks Like in Real Life

By example, the New Testament shows us what life in this spiritual family looks like in real life:

---

[51] See also Acts 4:23-31.

Acts 2:44-47

44 All the believers were together and had everything in common. 45 They sold property and possessions to give to anyone who had need. 46 Every day they continued to meet together in the temple courts. They broke bread in their homes and ate together with glad and sincere hearts, 47 praising God and enjoying the favor of all the people. And the Lord added to their number daily those who were being saved.

Acts 4:32-35

32 All the believers were one in heart and mind. No one claimed that any of their possessions was their own, but they shared everything they had. 33 With great power the apostles continued to testify to the resurrection of the Lord Jesus. And God's grace was so powerfully at work in them all 34 that there were no needy persons among them. For from time to time those who owned land or houses sold them, brought the money from the sales 35 and put it at the apostles' feet, and it was distributed to anyone who had need.

Note the emphases in these verses: "*all* the believers," "*everything*," and "*every* day." This way of life was the totality of their life! Their context required specific actions that may not be applicable in every situation; however, the love and devotion that compelled them to live in this manner is certainly universal. How might these thoughts regarding the believer's spiritual family relate to college relationships?

College Relationships

What does all of this talk about family and relationships have to do with the Christian college experience? First, a Christian education is best accomplished in a learning community, and community is all about relationships. Second, you will build relationships with your professors and school staff. Some of these people will become personal mentors to you. There is also the practical need for communication with them in matters related to your college program. Third, we are living in a day when many students do not come from a healthy family background, and Christian college has the potential to be the place where such students can experience life with a healthy spiritual family. Fourth, lifelong friendships can start here. Fifth, as an extension of the building of lifelong friendships, there is the possibility that lifelong marital relationships can have their start here at college.

A Learning Community

The greater matters of life pertaining to destiny are seldom accomplished alone. They are accomplished in community—doing life together. People need people in the fulfilling of their callings. No individual person has everything they need for the journey. I have something to contribute to your life, and you have something to contribute to mine. In the sharing of life together, we both are made richer in the process.

You and the other students around you are part of this learning community. College instructors and staff are part of it too, but the main emphasis here is the role that students play in the lives of one another. Christian students who have the Spirit of God dwelling within them are especially empowered to encourage, strengthen, edify and comfort one another.[52] The work of college academics can be difficult. Keep your eyes open for opportunities to speak life into someone else's difficult day. A timely word of Spirit-led affirmation may just change that person's life.

Your Professors and College Staff

As previously stated, your professors and college staff are here to set you up for success. They have devoted their lives to that end. While you may not always perceive them as buddies or close friends, generally they are educational professionals who genuinely care about you.

If you find yourself academically challenged, let your instructors know. If an instructor seems too busy to speak with you, then seek out help from other professionals at your college, such as your academic

---

[52] 1 Corinthians 14:3.

advisor or the director of the learning center. If you are uncertain who to contact, check with the Office of Academic Affairs.

If you face spiritual struggles, try reaching out to the campus chaplain or counselor. The dorm director may also be a person in whom you can confide. If you are uncertain who to contact regarding spiritual matters, the Dean of Students' office may be able to assist you.

Communication is the key in these relationships. Do you anticipate missing an upcoming class session? Are you going to be late submitting an assignment? Are you overdue turning in a paper? Are you concerned about your grades? Communicate with your professors. Do you need to drop a class? Are you going to be late on your next school payment? Are you confused about what classes you are supposed to take next semester? Communicate with the appropriate staff and administrative personnel. If they do not know about your concerns, they cannot help you.

While it is appropriate to emphasize the availability of college personnel, please remember that they are human. They may have their degrees and professional titles, but they are not superhuman. There will be limits to what they can actually do for you. They may not be able to meet with you at all hours of the day or night. Many of them have families at home, and all of them have scores or even hundreds of other students calling for their attention. Treat them with respect, honor and consideration.

Your Spiritual Family

Much has already been said about the spiritual family. If you are a born again believer, you are a member of God's family, whether you have accessed the full benefit of that identity or not. Your Christian college experience can become your opportunity to experience the benefit found in having spiritual fathers, mothers, sisters and brothers. As stated earlier, God has empowered *you* to take the initiative to reach out to someone in brotherly love.

Lifelong Friendships

In college you have the opportunity to establish new friendships with people who will remain friends for life. Let us consider a few suggestions for making new friends while in college.

1. Choose your friends wisely. Proverbs 13:20 says, "Walk with the wise and become wise, for a companion of fools suffers harm." Who are the people in your new environment who share your passion for Jesus and the things that are wholesome and good? Those are the people with whom you need to build relationships.

2. Spend more time around people. Be in the places on and around campus where other students gather, such as the student lounge, the cafeteria and other common areas. Attend sporting events and creative performances. Participate in school outings, student ministry excursions and community service projects. If you want to become known, you have to make yourself known by showing up in such places and at such times.

Someone once said, "You get to know people when you *work* with them, *play* with them and *pray* with them." Work together with others. Play together with them. Participate in student life events--times of fun and games. Pray together with others. Be regular and visibly present at chapel and prayer meetings. Do not sit in the back. Move toward the front and be immediately engaged in what is going on.

3. Utilize social networking. The responsible use of social media such as Facebook and Instagram can be good first step toward connecting with people on your campus. A friend request online can lead to an actual face-to-face conversation in the student lounge. If your first contact with a person is through social media, play it safe and make sure that your first face-to-face contact is in a public place.

4. Initiate conversation. Be the first one to break the awkward silence when you are with people that you do not know. Ask a question, or offer a sincere compliment. Introduce yourself, but do not monopolize the conversation by talking continuously about yourself. Aim to get the other person to talk, and demonstrate an attitude of interest as you listen. Be a good listener. Make an effort to remember things from the conversation so that the next time you meet that person, you can refer back to the previous conversation.

Where does one go in conversation once the typical introductory statements have been made? Try using the F.O.R.D. technique. F.O.R.D. is an acronym for Family, Occupation, Recreation and Dreams.

- **Family.** Start by asking about their family.
- **Occupation.** Ask questions about their occupation.
- **Recreation.** What do they enjoy doing for fun?
- **Dreams.** What are their dreams, aspirations and goals? What is ultimately important to them?

5. Focus on *being* a friend. Preoccupation with trying to get people to like *you* can come across as self-serving. If you go after *becoming* a friend to others, you will gain friends. There are lots of other people at your college who need a friend, and they are hoping that someone will reach out to them. Be that person who takes the first step toward helping someone else feel that they belong.

6. Be a *good* friend. Esteem others above yourself. Be caring. Be available. Be loyal.[53] Be reliable. Be trustworthy. Be an encourager. Be willing to make sacrifices for the sake of others. Be kind to everyone—even to those whom you are not trying to befriend.

7. Walk into every room with an other-oriented attitude. Do not enter thinking, "Here I am!" Instead enter with an attitude that says, "There you are!" Smile, emanate an attitude of joy, and make eye contact with everyone you meet.

8. Initiate times of getting together with others. If you are trying to befriend an individual, ask if they would like to get together for coffee. Often it is better to invite the person to join you or a group activity such as volleyball or hiking.

---

[53] Proverbs 17:17.

9. Pursue common interests. Friendships seem to work best if they are centered upon a common interest. Are you both interested in art? Visit an art gallery or art festival together. Do you both like sports? Go to an athletic event together.

10. Do not force yourself onto people. Know when to back away. Try not to take it personal when people do not seem interested in forming a friendship with you. That person may be facing difficult issues that you know nothing about.

Dating and Courtship

Christian college can be a great place to meet your future mate. Providing a detailed guide to dating and courtship is beyond the scope of this text; however, a few simple guidelines will be offered.

1. Consider the suggestions offered in the previous section on "Lifelong Friendships." Although dating and friendship are not the same thing, many of the foundational dynamics are the same. Some of the initial steps that a person may take toward a dating relationship resemble the initial steps for starting a new friendship.

2. Define the Relationship (DTR). The point may come early in the relationship where the two of you will need to discuss your mutual understanding of the relationship. Is this just a friendship? Are you exploring the possibilities of this relationship becoming a dating relationship? Are you both ready for the relationship to become a dating relationship or courtship? This mode of discussion is often referred to as a DTR (Define the Relationship). If you feel that this kind of discussion is needed, ask, "Do you mind if we have a DTR?"

3. Treat the other person with honor and respect. In this dating phase, you are laying a foundation for how you may (or may not) spend the rest of your life with this person. Ladies, this man is your brother in Christ. Gentlemen, this woman is your sister in Christ. Both of you are children of the King. Ladies, he is royalty. Gentlemen, she is royalty.

Here is another thought. Ladies, that young man is going to be someone's husband—maybe yours, or maybe someone else's. Be careful of how you relate to him, because there is a possibility that you may be interacting with someone else's future husband. Gentlemen, that young lady is going to be someone's wife—maybe yours, or maybe someone else's. Be careful of how you relate to her, because there is a possibility that you may be with someone else's future wife. If the two of you end up marrying someone else, you want to have a clear conscience knowing that you did nothing that was dishonoring or inappropriate with one another while you were dating. Even if the two of you do eventually become lifelong mates, you want to have a clear conscience regarding how you handled matters related to purity during your courtship.

Gentlemen, treating your date with honor and respect also involves some basic practices of etiquette. Open doors for her. Pay for meals and entertainment. Treat your date as a lady. Google the word "etiquette," and refresh your understanding of good manners.

4. Plan your date with a purpose. Both of you should know where you are going, what you are going to do and when you are returning. "Hanging out" is not a plan. Gentlemen, if you will plan your time with your date with a view toward wholesome enjoyment, you will demonstrate to her that you value and respect her. Ladies, if you will insist that the gentleman have a definite plan for the date, in so doing, he should sense your insistence upon integrity. Insistence upon a plan will protect both of you.

5. Keep love for Jesus your priority.[54] Jesus said, "If you love me, keep my commands."[55] Keep your love for Jesus and obedience to His commands at the center of your dating relationship. Both of you need

---

[54] Based on Stephen Altrogge, "Four Rules to Simplify Christian Dating," The Blazing Center: Connecting God's Truth to Real Life, accessed September 12, 2015, http://theblazingcenter.com/2014/08/four-rules-to-simplify-christian-dating.html.

[55] John 14:15.

to be devoted to Jesus. Dating an unbeliever should not be an option for a believer. The Bible instructs us to not be unequally yoked with unbelievers.[56]

6. Ask God for wisdom. The Bible says, "If any of you lacks wisdom, you should ask God, who gives generously to all without finding fault, and it will be given to you."[57] Wisdom is needed for responsible conduct in a dating relationship. Is it wise and responsible for a dating couple to go to secluded places alone? Would it be better to do things together publicly and with groups of people? Would it be best for the dating couple to ask a few mature believers to hold them accountable to Christian standards? Trust God for wisdom in these areas.

7. Pursue absolute purity.[58] The Bible instructs, "Flee from sexual immorality. All other sins a person commits are outside the body, but whoever sins sexually, sins against their own body."[59]

Premarital sex is definitely off-limits. Simulating sexual acts and making physical contact in a way that causes sexual arousal must also be regarded as off-limits. Is it wrong to kiss? Each couple must carefully navigate such matters with wisdom and with a resolve to live a pure life. If the physical activity triggers runaway passions racing toward sexual contact, stop! For some, a kiss may be okay, but for others, kissing may need to be off limits.

8. Cultivate community.[60] A dating couple should not neglect fellowship or community with other believers. When you are dating, do not become so preoccupied with one another that you find yourself shutting out the rest of the human race. Friends and family are still

---

[56] 2 Corinthians 6:14.

[57] James 1:5.

[58] Based on Stephen Altrogge's previously cited work.

[59] 1 Corinthians 6:18.

[60] Based on Stephen Altrogge's previously cited work.

important. Pursue community, and allow other trusted individuals to speak wisdom into your life regarding your dating relationship.

9. Become familiar with your college's guidelines for dating. What is your school's position regarding public displays of affection (PDA)? Are there other guidelines of which you need to be made aware? Check your Student Handbook.

10. Stay teachable. Learn as much as you can about this subject. An excellent resource for young adults is Moral Revolution—a ministry developed by some of the leaders of Bethel Church in Redding, California. Visit moralrevolution.com.

Divine Order for Relationships

Some people are strongly individualistic, thinking that they can go after their dreams in solo mode. In other words, they feel that they do not need anyone else's involvement in their journey. They think that they can do it all by themselves. God did not design life to even work properly in solo mode. We were built for community. We need one another. My strengths are intended to offset someone else's weaknesses, and my weaknesses may require the aid of someone else's strength. It is worth repeating: the greater matters of life related to personal destiny are accomplished in community. You cannot do it alone.

All of life is about relationships, and Christian college is a place where divine order for relationships, communication and conflict resolution should be taught and modeled. The Bible contains a wealth of instructions on how believers should relate to one another. In the space provided beneath each passage in the following exercise, write your own reflections concerning the verse's implications for your relationships. You may also use the space to take notes from your instructor's comments.

Accept One Another

Romans 15:7

Accept one another, then, just as Christ accepted you, in order to bring praise to God.

Admonish One Another

Colossians 3:16

Let the word of Christ dwell in you richly as you teach and admonish one another with all wisdom, and as you sing psalms, hymns and spiritual songs with gratitude in your hearts to God.

Bear One Another's Burdens

Galatians 6:2

Carry each other's burdens, and in this way you will fulfill the law of Christ.

Bear with One Another

Ephesians 4:2

Be completely humble and gentle; be patient, bearing with one another in love.

Confess Faults to One Another

James 5:16
Therefore confess your sins to each other and pray for each other so that you may be healed. The prayer of a righteous man is powerful and effective.

Be Devoted to One Another

Romans 12:10a
Be devoted to one another in brotherly love.

Encourage One Another

1 Thessalonians 5:11
Therefore encourage one another and build each other up, just as in fact you are doing.

Fellowship with One Another

1 John 1:7
But if we walk in the light, as He is in the light, we have fellowship with one another.

Forgive One Another

Ephesians 4:32
Be kind and compassionate to one another, forgiving each other, just as in Christ God forgave you.

Be Honest with One Another

Colossians 3:9
Do not lie to each other, since you have taken off your old self with its practices.

Honor One Another

Romans 12:10b
Honor one another above yourselves.

Be Hospitable to One Another

1 Peter 4:9
Offer hospitality to one another without grumbling.

Be Kind to One Another

Ephesians 4:32
Be kind and compassionate to one another, forgiving each other, just as in Christ God forgave you.

Members One of Another

Romans 12:5
So in Christ we who are many form one body, and each member belongs to all the others.

Be of the Same Mind with One Another

Romans 15:5
May the God who gives endurance and encouragement give you a spirit of unity among yourselves[61] as you follow Christ Jesus.

Submit to One Another

Ephesians 5:21
Submit to one another out of reverence for Christ.

---

[61] In Romans 15:5, "A spirit of unity among yourselves" can also be rendered "the same mind among each other."

Serve One Another

Galatians 5:13

You, my brothers, were called to be free. But do not use your freedom to indulge the sinful nature; rather, serve one another in love.

Spur One Another On

Hebrews 10:24

And let us consider how we may spur one another on toward love and good deeds.

Serve One Another

Galatians 5:13

You, my brothers, were called to be free. But do not use your freedom to indulge the sinful nature; rather, serve one another in love.

Pray for One Another

James 5:16

Therefore confess your sins to each other and pray for each other so that you may be healed. The prayer of a righteous man is powerful and effective.

Love One Another

The exhortation to "love one another" binds together the whole body of the "one another" doctrine. The call to love one another occurs at least eleven times in the New Testament. In the space beneath each passage below, comment on the implications for *your* relationships. You may also use this area to take notes from your instructor's remarks.

Love One Another

John 13:34
"A new command I give you: Love one another. As I have loved you, so you must love one another."

John 13:35
"By this everyone will know that you are my disciples, if you love one another."

Romans 13:8
Let no debt remain outstanding, except the continuing debt to love one another, for whoever loves others has fulfilled the law.

1 Peter 1:22

Now that you have purified yourselves by obeying the truth so that you have sincere love for each other, love one another deeply, from the heart.

1 Peter 3:8

Finally, all of you, be like-minded, be sympathetic, love one another, be compassionate and humble.

1 John 3:11

For this is the message you heard from the beginning: We should love one another.

1 John 3:23

And this is his command: to believe in the name of his Son, Jesus Christ, and to love one another as he commanded us.

1 John 4:7
Dear friends, let us love one another, for love comes from God. Everyone who loves has been born of God and knows God.

1 John 4:11
Dear friends, since God so loved us, we also ought to love one another.

1 John 4:12
No one has ever seen God; but if we love one another, God lives in us and his love is made complete in us.

2 John 1:5
And now, dear lady, I am not writing you a new command but one we have had from the beginning. I ask that we love one another.

Gateway to the Christian College Experience

1 Corinthians 13:1-13
1 If I speak in the tongues of men or of angels, but do not have love, I am only a resounding gong or a clanging cymbal.
2 If I have the gift of prophecy and can fathom all mysteries and all knowledge, and if I have a faith that can move mountains, but do not have love, I am nothing.
3 If I give all I possess to the poor and give over my body to hardship that I may boast, but do not have love, I gain nothing.

4 Love is patient,

love is kind.

It does not envy,

it does not boast,

it is not proud.

5 It does not dishonor others,

it is not self-seeking,

it is not easily angered,

it keeps no record of wrongs.

6 Love does not delight in evil but rejoices with the truth

7 It always protects,

always trusts,

always hopes,

always perseveres.

8 Love never fails. But where there are prophecies, they will cease; where there are tongues, they will be stilled; where there is knowledge, it will pass away.
9 For we know in part and we prophesy in part,
10 but when completeness comes, what is in part disappears. 11 When I was a child, I talked like a child, I thought like a child, I reasoned like a child. When I became a man, I put the ways of childhood behind me.
12 For now we see only a reflection as in a mirror; then we shall see face to face. Now I know in part; then I shall know fully, even as I am fully known.

> 13 And now these three remain: faith, hope and love. But the greatest of these is love.

Confrontation and Criticism

Honoring one another is an important part of college life. However, a culture of honor must also include the freedom to confront negative interpersonal issues in a healthy manner. To honor another person does not mean that their unbecoming attitudes and behavior may go unchecked. Honor must not allow an "anything goes" mindset to creep into the environment.

When confronting something that is not right, criticize the behavior, not the person. Be specific about the perceived problem. Allow time for the person to respond. Once they have responded, you may discover that you have misunderstood the situation. If the person does prove to be at fault, look for an opportunity to offer help. Be as positive in your approach as possible, and approach everything from a mindset of hope—expect a favorable outcome.

When you are the recipient of criticism, listen, hold on to the true, and flush the rest. In humility, you may want to ask for suggestions on how to change your behavior. Whatever you do, do not throw more fuel on the fire. If you have cultivated a lifestyle of hosting God's presence, then release peace into the situation.

State three key insights gained from this chapter that seemed especially relevant to your Christian college experience.

Chapter 10
Finishing Strong

As you approach the end of a semester, it is important to be intentional about finishing strong. Anticipation of the Christmas break or the summer break can be a distraction causing the mind and emotions to detach from the academic work at hand. Stay focused, and determine to be at your best as you approach the finish line. Consider the following tips for finishing your semester strong:

1. **Go to class.** Showing up for class should be the obvious thing to do, but the temptation to do otherwise can be compelling as you approach the end of the semester.

2. **Treat college work like a job.** [62] How would you treat your job? Hopefully you would be there on time or even early. You would also want to give it your very best effort. Approach your college work with the same spirit of excellence.

3. **Know your status.** Know where you stand. Review your syllabus. Check your college's online Learning Management System. Take responsibility for yourself.

4. **Communicate with your instructors.** What information do you need from them? What do they need from you? Be proactive; take the initiative to communicate.

5. **Put study time ahead of social time.** However, with discipline you can reward yourself with short segments of

---

[62] Tips one and two are based on "How to Finish the Semester Strong," Go Ennounce: It's Cool 2 Talk School, November 14, 2014, accessed September 12, 2015, http://blog.goennounce.com/how-to-finish-the-semester-strong/.

time with your friends, after you have accomplished specific academic goals.

6. **Do not cram.** Pace yourself throughout the entire semester to prevent everything from piling up at the end.

7. **Clean off your desk.** A cluttered desk clutters the mind. Put everything out of sight except for the items needed for the day's work.

8. **Make a list.** [63] Go through the syllabi you received for your classes to identify essential tasks that must be completed before the end of the semester. Review your calendar and assignment descriptions as well. Create a master list, and number the items according to their priority or according to the chronological order in which the tasks must be accomplished.

9. **Stay healthy.** Take occasional walks, and maintain an exercise routine. Monitor what you eat. Get at least seven hours of sleep each night. [64] Keep yourself properly hydrated. Avoid sugar; try replacing candy and snacks with frequent drinks of water.

10. **Tend to your spiritual life.** In the midst of end-of-semester stresses, it is especially important to remain strong in spirit. Stay centered on the presence of God by frequently turning your affections toward Him. Do not neglect prayer. Meditate on the Scriptures. Give thanks continually.

---

[63] Tips seven and eight are based on Shawn Christ, "Tips on How to Finish Out the Semester Strong," November 27, 2013, accessed September 12, 2015, http://onwardstate.com/ 2012/ 11/ 27/ tips-on-how-to-finish-out-the-semester-strong/.

[64] Tips three through six and tip nine are based in part on "Ending Your Semester Strong," Gateway Technical College, accessed September 12, 2015, https://www.gtc.edu/multicultural-program/ending-your-semester-strong.

Concluding Reflections

As this portion of your college experience draws to a close, consider what you have learned. What has God spoken to you? What do you anticipate God doing in your life in your remaining time in college? In the space provided below, note your response to these questions. Then write a prayer concerning the college days that yet await you.

What has God spoken to you this semester / quarter?

Gateway to the Christian College Experience

What do you anticipate God doing in your life in your remaining time in college?

Write a short prayer regarding the remainder of your time in college.

Made in the USA
Charleston, SC
13 January 2017